This Thing Called Literature

T0372524

What is this thing called literature? Why study it? And how?

Relating literature to topics such as dreams, politics, life, death, the ordinary and the uncanny, *This Thing Called Literature* establishes a sense of why and how literature is an exciting and rewarding subject to study. Andrew Bennett and Nicholas Royle expertly weave an essential love of literature into an account of what literary texts do, how they work and the sort of questions and ideas they provoke.

The book's three parts reflect the fundamental components of studying literature: reading, thinking and writing. The authors use helpful and wide-ranging examples and summaries, offering rich reflections on the question 'What is literature?' and on what they term 'creative reading'. The new edition has been revised throughout with extensive updates to the further reading and a new chapter on creative non-fiction.

Bennett and Royle's accessible and thought-provoking style encourages a deep engagement with literary texts. This essential guide to the study of literature is an eloquent celebration of the value and pleasure of reading.

Andrew Bennett is Professor of English at the University of Bristol, UK. He publishes on Romantic and twentieth-century literature and on literary theory. His books include *An Introduction to Literature, Criticism, and Theory, Sixth Edition* (2023; with Nicholas Royle), *Suicide Century: Literature and Suicide from James Joyce to David Foster Wallace* (2017) and *Ignorance: Literature and Agnoiology* (2009).

Nicholas Royle is Professor Emeritus of English at the University of Sussex, UK. He is the author of many critical books, including *How to Read Shakespeare* (2014) and *Veering: A Theory of Literature* (2011), as well as creative works such as *An English Guide to Birdwatching* (2017) and *David Bowie, Enid Blyton and the Sun Machine* (2023).

'Combining a precis of literary theory with advice on how to read and write creatively, *This Thing Called Literature*, the third book from Andrew Bennett and Nicholas Royle, is a neat little guide for undergraduates, or anyone who wants to know more about literary studies. It is the kind of book tutors and lecturers could enjoy and learn from, as well as their students.'

Rachel Darling, *TLS*

'Clear, fair-minded, and patiently elaborating, this is an invaluable field guide for seasoned teachers and scholars as well as beginning students.'

Wai Chee Dimock, *William Lampson Professor of English and American Studies, Yale University, USA*

'*This Thing Called Literature* is another triumph by Andrew Bennett and Nicholas Royle. They are our most trusted guides to literary study writing today. Their exemplary pedagogy opens up the wonders and complexity of both literature and study itself. The future of reading has been given a fighting chance by this wonderful book, which will benefit everyone who reads it from the A Level student to the Emeritus Professor.'

Martin McQuillan, *Professor and Director of ICE, Edge Hill University, UK*

'What the duo of Strunk and White is to writing well, the duo of Bennett and Royle is to reading carefully and, especially, to thinking deeply about literature. *This Thing Called Literature* is a fun, fresh take on why we study literature and how to do it, and is a useful and accessible read for students just beginning their study; it is also a rewarding, heartening read for those of us who got into the business of literary study for the love of reading, thinking, and writing.'

Daniel Robinson, *Homer C. Nearing Jr. Distinguished Professor of English, Widener University, USA*

'Reports on the so-called "death of literature" – its increasing irrelevance in an age of digital reason – are, we have long suspected, greatly exaggerated. Andrew Bennett and Nicholas Royle confirm this with a timely and robust case for the defence, repositioning literary studies at the centre of the humanities. With their eloquent readings, witty *aperçus* and compendious range of reference, the authors provide the kinds of insightful pleasures that, they argue, are central to the literary arts themselves. The book's brevity is no indication of its ambition: if *This Thing Called Literature* does not make you a better reader, writer, critic and thinker, you haven't been reading it closely enough.'

Paul Sheehan, *Associate Professor in English, Macquarie University, Sydney, Australia*

This Thing Called Literature

Reading, Thinking, Writing

Second edition

ANDREW BENNETT AND
NICHOLAS ROYLE

Routledge
Taylor & Francis Group

LONDON AND NEW YORK

Designed cover image: © Kabe Wilson, detail from Skyline 5.18pm, oil on canvas, 2007

Second edition published 2024
by Routledge
4 Park Square, Milton Park, Abingdon, Oxon, OX14 4RN

and by Routledge
605 Third Avenue, New York, NY 10158

Routledge is an imprint of the Taylor & Francis Group, an informa business

First edition published by Routledge 2015

British Library Cataloguing-in-Publication Data
A catalogue record for this book is available from the British Library

ISBN: 978-1-032-29379-0 (hbk)
ISBN: 978-1-032-28584-9 (pbk)
ISBN: 978-1-003-30136-3 (ebk)

DOI: 10.4324/9781003301363

Typeset in Bembo
by Apex CoVantage, LLC

Contents

List of figures   ix
Acknowledgements   x

1   Studying literature   1

PART I
Reading   **19**

2   Reading a poem   21
3   Reading a novel   35
4   Reading a short story   50
5   Reading a play   60
6   Reading creative non-fiction   72

PART II
Thinking   **87**

7   Thinking about literature   89
8   Thinking critically   101

PART III
Writing   **113**

9   Writing an essay   115

10   Creative writing: the impossible   129
11   Writing short fiction   136

     Appendix: the wordbook   145
     Glossary   148
     Bibliography   157
     Index   168

Figures

2.1 Pieter Brueghel (c.1527–69), *Landscape with the Fall of Icarus* (1569).   25

3.1 Title-page to Daniel Defoe, *Robinson Crusoe*, first edition (London, 1719).   39

3.2 Title-page to Daniel Defoe, *Moll Flanders*, first edition (London, 1721 [1722]).   40

7.1 George Herbert, *The Temple: Sacred Poems and Private Ejaculations* (Cambridge, 1633), pp. 34–35.   94

Acknowledgements

'Funeral Blues', Copyright © 1940 by W.H. Auden, renewed. Reprinted by permission of Curtis Brown, Ltd. All rights reserved.

'Funeral Blues', copyright 1940 and © renewed 1968 by W.H. Auden; from COLLECTED POEMS by W. H. Auden, edited by Edward Mendelson. Used by permission of Random House, an imprint and division of Penguin Random House LLC. All rights reserved.

'Musée des Beaux Arts', Copyright © 1939 by W.H. Auden. Reprinted by permission of Curtis Brown, Ltd. All rights reserved.

'Musée des Beaux Arts', copyright 1940 and © renewed 1968 by W. H. Auden; from COLLECTED POEMS by W. H. Auden, edited by Edward Mendelson. Used by permission of Random House, an imprint and division of Penguin Random House LLC. All rights reserved.

'Hawk Roosting" from *Lupercal* by Ted Hughes. Copyright © 2003 by The Estate of Ted Hughes Reprinted by permission of Faber and Faber Ltd.

'Aubade' from *The Complete Poems* of Philip Larkin, edited by Archie Burnett. Reprinted by permission of Faber and Faber Ltd.

Every effort has been made to contact copyright holders of material reproduced in this product. We would be pleased to rectify any omissions should they be drawn to our attention.

1. Studying literature

In this book we hope to give a sense of why and how literature might be an exciting and rewarding subject to study. Our primary concern is with a love of literature, with what literary texts do, with how they work and what sorts of questions and ideas they provoke. Our aim is to be concise, to give pleasure and to provide a clear and stimulating account of studying literature.

The book is primarily written for people who are starting, or who are thinking about starting, literary studies at college or university. We begin at the beginning, with the questions: 'What is literature?' and 'Why study it?' We then have a series of chapters on the three basic activities involved in studying literature: reading, thinking and writing. Part I comprises short chapters on reading a poem, reading a novel, reading a short story, reading a play and reading creative non-fiction. Part II considers the question 'What is thinking?' – especially as regards thinking in and about literature and thinking critically. Part III turns to questions of writing. There are chapters on how to write an essay, on creative writing and on writing short fiction.

What is this thing called literature?

This is a question to which no one has yet provided an entirely satisfactory or convincing answer. As the critic Raymond Williams observes in a discussion of this question in his book *Keywords*, literature is 'a difficult word, in part because its conventional contemporary meaning appears, at first sight, so simple' (Williams 1983, 183). The hedging precision of

DOI: 10.4324/9781003301363-1

Williams's phrasing ('in part', 'appears', 'at first sight') points towards the complexity of the question.

It is possible to provide numerous cogent but ultimately unsatisfactory answers to the question 'What is literature?' We might start with a couple of dictionary definitions, along with an observation about the recent historical and institutional significance of the term 'literature'. *Chambers* dictionary, for example, gives (1) 'the art of composition in prose and verse' and (2) 'literary matter' as two senses of the word 'literature'. And since the late nineteenth century, 'literature' has been understood to mean a subject of study in schools and universities, involving certain kinds of imaginative or creative writing, including fiction, poetry and drama.

As we hope to make clear in this book, however, 'literature' is a peculiarly elusive word. It has, in a sense, no essence. With a bit of effort and imagination, we would suggest, any text *can* be read as poetic – the list of ingredients on a box of breakfast cereal, for example, or even the most inane language of bureaucracy. Anything at all that happens, in the world or in your head, can be imagined as 'drama'. And fiction (or storytelling) has a funny and perhaps irresistible way of getting mixed up with its alleged opposite ('real life', 'the real world').

While we attempt, in the pages ahead, to clarify what may seem enigmatic and perplexing about the nature of our subject (the study of 'literature'), we are also concerned to stay true to it – in other words, to foreground and keep in mind what is slippery and strange about literature. Rather than strive for definitive answers and a final sense of certainty in this context, we want to suggest that there is value in the very experiences of uncertainty to which the question 'What is this thing called literature?' gives rise.

Uncertainty is, moreover, a consistent and powerful factor *in* literary texts themselves: literary works – especially those most valued or considered most 'classic' or canonical – are themselves full of difficult, even impossible questions. We might consider just three memorable and enduring questions that occur in literary works. First, there is what is perhaps the most famous line in all of Shakespeare's writings, Hamlet's 'To be, or not to be; that is the question' (3.1.58). Second, in Charles Dickens's *Oliver Twist* (1838), the young Oliver, desperately hungry, asks his master for more gruel: 'Please, sir, I want some more' (Dickens 2003, 15). Finally, there is the marvellously odd (funny-strange and funny-amusing) poem by Emily Dickinson, written in about 1861, which begins: 'I'm Nobody! Who are you? / Are you – Nobody – Too?'

(Dickinson 1975, Poem 288). None of these is a simple question or, indeed, simply a question. Let us expand briefly on each of these examples.

In the case of Shakespeare's *Hamlet* (1600–1), we only know that 'to be or not to be' is supposed to be heard as a question rather than understood as the specification of an alternative (either 'to be', to live, to carry on being, or to stop, to commit suicide, to not be), because Hamlet tells us so. We think of Hamlet as a word-man, associating him for instance with the celebrated phrase 'words, words, words' (his equivocal answer to Polonius's deceptively straightforward question 'What do you read, my lord?': 2.2.193–94). But when Hamlet says 'To be, or not to be', he is not merely playing with words. Rather he is posing a question that is a matter literally of life or death. And this question is about the desire to die. It is 'a consummation', as Hamlet goes on to say, '[d]evoutly to be wished' (3.1.65–66).

The question resonates throughout the play and indeed continues to resonate today. What is this desire for self-destruction? Is it in some strange way peculiarly human? Or is it, as Sigmund Freud seems to suppose in his discussion of the death drive in *Beyond the Pleasure Principle* (1920), inherent in all life forms? How does literature illuminate these questions and help us to think critically about self-destruction, not only in the context of the life of an individual (the self-destructiveness of drug addiction or self-harm, for example, or other damaging, obsessive behaviour) but also with regard to the behaviour of communities, societies or states more generally (the apparent blind determination to destroy the environment, for instance; to maintain the alleged purity of some ethnic, racial or nationalist identity; or to seek revenge even or perhaps especially to one's own detriment).

There is something similarly urgent and real at stake in Oliver's request for more food. 'Please, sir, I want some more' is, strictly speaking, not formulated as a question, with an interrogative tone or question mark at the end, but it is certainly understood as asking for *something*. Mr Bumble, his master, 'a fat, healthy man', responds by exclaiming 'What!' in 'stupified astonishment', then hitting the little boy on the head with a copper ladle and reporting the matter to Mr Limbkins and other members of the Board: '"Oliver Twist has asked for more." There was a general start. Horror was depicted on every countenance' (Dickens 2003, 15). The eight-year-old's request is shocking and ironic in ways that ramify across Dickens's novel and continue to provoke questions. What does it mean, how is it possible, for a beneficiary of charity to ask for *more*? How does this request disturb the relationship between donor and donee? If Dickens lets a sort of grim humour play over the scene, it is principally in order to underscore the sense of outrage. For Bumble himself, the little boy's question is evidence for his prediction that 'that boy will be hung', and the very next morning he has a bill 'pasted on the outside of the gate, offering a reward of five pounds to anybody who would take Oliver Twist off the hands of the parish' (15). The boy's question, in other words, has disturbingly physical and violent consequences. At the same time, we are made aware of the force of a question that resounds down the years and is still with us: Why should any child be 'desperate with hunger and reckless with misery' (15)? Why should any child, in England or anywhere else in the world, be forced to beg and be punished for doing so?

Finally, Emily Dickinson's lines involve not one but a sort of double question that also entails an enigmatic and unsettling affirmation ('I'm Nobody!'). Moreover, the poet plays with capitalization and punctuation in ways that make questions proliferate within each question. We are prompted to wonder, for example: is 'Nobody' a proper name? Is Dickinson, in capitalizing the 'too', suggesting that 'Too' is a proper name too? What is a name in fact? Would you be someone if you didn't have a name? Are we justified in supposing that it is truly the poet who is addressing us? In what sense is the poet, any poet, a 'nobody'? Is there a wry allusion here to John Keats's celebrated remark that a poet is like a 'cameleon' and has 'no self' (see Keats 2005, 60)? Who is the poet addressing here? Is it me? Am I nobody, too? And how do the dashes affect our sense of where Dickinson's questions start – or stop?

One of the strange things about a literary work is its very uncertainty. And literature can always be read *otherwise*. At issue is an experience of uncertainty that goes to the heart of the law, entailing issues of property and identity. Many contemporary novels carry a cautionary note or disclaimer on the back (the 'verso') of the title-page. Don DeLillo's *Point Omega* (2010), for example, specifies: 'This book is a work of fiction. Names, characters, places, and incidents either are products of the author's imagination or are used fictitiously. Any resemblance to actual events or locales or persons, living or dead, is entirely coincidental.'

How seriously are we supposed to take this? DeLillo's novel makes reference to *Psycho* (1960, dir. Alfred Hitchcock), to Anthony Perkins and Janet Leigh, to New York City and to the Pentagon, as well as to the enormity of so-called 'extraordinary rendition'. Is 'the Pentagon' in DeLillo's book *nothing to do with* the Pentagon that we all know about, the US military headquarters in Washington, DC? Are the Anthony Perkins or Janet Leigh to which the book alludes *completely different* from the actors who appear in Hitchcock's world-famous movie? Is the precise, rather chilling discussion of the word 'rendition' in the book just 'fictitious', even when it is informing the reader about 'enhanced interrogation techniques' and the history of the word ('*rendition* – a giving up or giving back . . . Old French, Obsolete French and torture by proxy') (DeLillo 2010, 33)? And, anyway, what does 'entirely coincidental' mean? Coincidence is a compelling and decisive element in fictional writing, whether this is construed as 'true chance' or 'fate masquerading as chance' (Jordan 2010, xiii), but the 'entirely' here seems to over-egg the pudding. To borrow the words of Shakespeare's Ophelia, the author's disclaimer 'protests too much, methinks' (*Hamlet*, 3.2.219).

Other contemporary novelists have noticed the strangeness of the so-called 'copyright page'. In the 'Author's Foreword' to David Foster Wallace's *The Pale King* (2011), for example, the speaker (allegedly Wallace himself) resolutely denies that the book is 'fiction at all', arguing that it is 'more like a memoir than any kind of made-up story' and that therefore the 'only bona fide "fiction" here is the copyright page's disclaimer' (Wallace 2011, 67–68). The only purpose of the disclaimer, Wallace adds, is as a 'legal device' to 'protect me, the book's publisher, and the publisher's assigned distributors from legal liability' (68). The disclaimer, in other words, is 'a lie' (69). But is it a lie? How can we tell? Is this David Foster Wallace the 'real' David Foster Wallace, or is he a character in a book?

The seemingly dull back of the title-page of a novel, then, becomes a good deal less certain than one might have supposed. 'This book', we are told, 'is a work of fiction'. But this *part* of the book (the information on the back of the title-page) is *not* part of the book. If this sounds slightly unhinged, that's because it is. Various bits of the text, including the title and the name of the author, are crucial to the novel's being legally designated as a novel, 'a work of fiction', without necessarily being part of the novel as such. Is the title of a novel part or not part of the novel it entitles? The answer is less straightforward than one might hope. It is both and neither.

As these reflections might suggest, even a disclaimer about a novel not, in effect, having anything to do with the real world has serious implications for what we think the real world is, for how we think about where the literary nature of a text begins or stops or, conversely, about where law (legal claims of property and copyright, the determination of who or what is 'real' and 'actual' and so on) separates from fiction. Even (or perhaps especially) when people try to make declarations or stipulations about what is *not* literature, the question with which we began ('What is this thing called literature?') comes back to haunt.

What is the point of studying literature?

The world is in an absolutely terrible state and people want to talk about *poems* and *novels* and *plays* and other sorts of *creative writing*? If I am going to study something, aren't there more pressing or more practical subjects, such as physics or medicine or law or politics? Where does studying literature take me? What can I do with it?

You have perhaps asked these questions yourself or heard others ask them. In this book we attempt to provide some answers. Some of our answers take the form of one-liners. Others involve a more patient and detailed elaboration. Either way, we will see that answers also raise further questions and indeed that developing *the art of questioning* is one of the rewards or special effects of literary study.

If we were to play the role of devil's advocate, we might say: there is *no obvious point* in studying literature. It seems to serve no purpose. It leads directly to no career or vocation, unless you want to become a teacher or researcher in literary studies who teaches and researches something that has no obvious point, seems to serve no purpose and so on, round in a circle. In fact, for a budding poet or novelist it is not even clear that studying literature is more helpful than studying medicine, say, or mechanical engineering. From the perspective of professional training or practical knowledge, literary studies is a dead-end. It's a non-starter.

However – or *contrariwise*, as Tweedledee might say (see Carroll 1992, 146) – it is precisely this apparent purposelessness that makes the study of literature interesting. Unlike more or less every other thing you have to do in life that is connected with studying or working for a living, the study of literature doesn't tie you down to anything. It frees you up. It opens up remarkable possibilities.

Literary studies is often seen as lacking the intellectual rigour of a subject like philosophy, where you are at least supposed to train your thinking and learn about the limits of knowledge, about philosophical systems, about the meaning of existence, about formal logic and so on. And literary studies is also often seen as lacking the seriousness and dignity of history, from the study of which you are supposed to acquire a sound understanding of the past based on careful investigation of manuscripts, artefacts, archival records and other data. As a university subject, literature is the odd one out, the weird one: it often seems that governments and university managers alike don't really know what to do with it. But precisely because it has no obvious point, it is for some the most alluring of all subjects to study: more than any other discipline, literary studies is a space of intellectual freedom, open to imagination, experimentation and exploration.

The exploration is focused, first of all, on language itself. What does 'space' mean here, and 'freedom'? Are these terms literal or figurative? Is this about 'freedom of speech' or 'physical freedom' or something else? What is this 'space of literature' (to use Maurice Blanchot's compelling phrase (1982))? Literature can be about *anything* and can therefore teach us *anything* – its possibilities and potential are endless.

The sky is not the limit

We might think about this in terms of the sky. If the study of literature is concerned with what people call blue-sky thinking, it is also concerned with red-sky, black-sky and no-sky thinking. 'Red sky' conventionally connotes a beautiful day to come ('Red sky at night, shepherd's delight') or a sense of impending danger such as a storm ('Red sky at morning, shepherds take warning'): literary studies is concerned with aesthetic beauty ('shepherd's delight'), but also with what is threatening or dangerous. Literature is a place not only for fine language, lovely images and positive sorts of aesthetic experience ('Isn't this poem *beautiful?*') but also for what is disturbing, menacing, even terrifying. We find ourselves drawn into 'black sky thinking': literature is very often explicitly about suffering, melancholy, death and tragedy ('Isn't this play *disturbing?*'). Poems, plays and novels can take us into very dark places. Some would say that they do so in ways that are richer and more illuminating, stranger and more instructive than is the case with other disciplines, such as psychology or philosophy.

And then you may be wondering: '*No sky* thinking', did they say? What are they talking about? The writings of Samuel Beckett, in particular, seem to us preoccupied with the notion of 'no sky' thinking – thinking in a claustrophobically enclosed place, thinking in the dark or thinking in which a 'cloudless sky' is occluded by a 'clouded pane': such kinds of thinking are evident in his novel *The Unnamable* (1953), the late prose text *Company* (1980) and the very late prose fragment 'Stirrings Still' (1989), respectively. More broadly, we can think about the question of literature in terms of realism and verisimilitude. We might illustrate this by reference to the front cover of *This Thing Called Literature*. It is a picture of a sunset. It may look like a photograph, but it is actually a painting. The artist, Kabe Wilson, has painted this sky into existence. Correspondingly, no sky in a literary text is an actual sky. Realism is a form of fiction. Verisimilitude is artifice. (We will say more about realism and verisimilitude shortly.)

For literary studies, then, the sky is not the limit, although it might be a particularly remarkable subject for analysis and reflection. As the poet Wallace Stevens says in one of his essays, 'when we look at the blue sky for the first time, that is to say: not merely see it, but look at it and experience it', it is only then that we can begin to appreciate that 'we live in the centre of a physical poetry' (Stevens 1951, 65–66). In this sense, literature *makes it new* (to recall a phrase that Ezra Pound uses to describe the Modernist mood in 1928: see North 2013, 162–169). It allows us to see the world differently, 'purging' from our 'inward sight', as the Romantic poet Percy Bysshe Shelley put it in 1821, the 'film of familiarity which obscures from us the wonder of our being' (Shelley 1977, 505).

Literature and other worlds

A literary work, it is often said, is a work of imagination. It takes us into another world, whether this is construed as another version of *this* world or as somewhere *out of this world*, beyond the world, unearthly. Literature is thus about other worlds or transformations of the world we know. From this perspective it might even be said that revolutionary changes in the world always entail a literary dimension. It is not by chance that we refer to major events as 'dramatic' – precisely as if, in the words of Shakespeare's *As You Like It*, 'All the world's a stage' (2.7.139). And if we think about major events and their aftermaths – the fall of the Soviet Union, 9/11, the invention of the internal combustion engine or the smart phone, the abolition of slavery, the decriminalization of homosexuality (at least in many countries) or the COVID-19 pandemic – these often have an element of the dream-like or incredible. 'Was it really like that before? It seems unimaginable now' and so on.

The past is in many respects like a dream. At the same time, dreams and literary texts have a great deal in common. By this we are thinking not only of dream visions in medieval poetry (such as *Piers Plowman* or *Pearl*) and other literary representations of sleep and dreaming, but more generally about the dream-like logic and structure of literary works. Like dreams, they are full of sudden alterations of place and perspective, strange or unlikely characters showing up, coincidences and reversals, as well as words and phrases unexpectedly pregnant with meaning.

Politics of literature, literature of politics

This is not to suggest that literature is merely escapist or fanciful. If literature is dream-like, it is also worldly, political through and through. Studying literature can make you a 'political animal' in surprising ways. Literary works invite you to think about *context*. They prompt questions that range from the obvious to the more enigmatic. On the obvious side, then, we wonder: When was this text written and published? Who wrote it? What genre or genres does it belong to? What is it seeking to tell us and why? In what cultural, social, political context was it produced? What cultural, social, political issues does it encourage us to think about? And on the less obvious side: Why does a play written in 1599, such as Shakespeare's *Julius Caesar*, seem to have more to tell us about sovereignty and democracy today than any number of contemporary, ostensibly more explicit novels on such topics? What are the limits of 'cultural, social, political context'?

In the second half of the twentieth century, critics used to talk of 'formalism' and 'New Criticism' as terms referring to ways of reading poems and other artworks without needing to engage with questions of context. You were presented with the poem on the page, and that was all you needed to consider. No text exists in splendid isolation, however: everything is connected. We are living in what Amitav Ghosh calls 'a world of insistent, inescapable continuities' (Ghosh 2016, 62). Even the notion of 'cultural context' becomes questionable for, as Timothy Clark points out, 'culture itself has a context – the biosphere, air, water, plant and animal life – and [these issues] involve perspectives or questions for which given cultural conceptions seem limited' (Clark 2011, 4). Worldly and political concerns pervade literature, even (or especially) if a writer or critic claims otherwise.

To turn this idea around, we can see that even the 'political sphere' in its most traditional form is unthinkable without literary dimensions, such as storytelling, rhetorical tropes, dramatizing and other poetic effects. The most important and enduring political statements themselves have literary qualities. Today's politicians might seem more than ever a bunch of corporate, cliché-touting, party puppets, but even they know that a good speech – or even a single memorably fine phrase – can make or save a career. Great *political* texts invariably carry a *poetic* charge. 'A spectre is haunting Europe' (the opening words of the *Communist Manifesto*, written by Karl Marx and Friedrich Engels in 1848) is hardly an everyday, prosaic remark. The same goes for Martin Luther King's brilliantly anaphoric 'I have a dream . . .' speech in Washington, DC, in August 1963. As one of the Situationists (a group of European avant-garde revolutionaries) observed in the same year: 'Every revolution has been born in poetry, has first of all been made with the force of poetry' (see Knabb 2006, 150–151).

In his poem 'In Memory of W.B. Yeats' (1939), W.H. Auden gloomily declared that poetry 'makes nothing happen' (Auden 1979, 82), but in the domain of politics, as elsewhere, the study of literature provides a sharper understanding of the poetic as, precisely, a doing or making. The ancient Greek origin of the word 'poetry', after all, is the verb *poiein*: to make or to do (the national poet of Scotland is still called the 'Makar'). Politicians (with the help of their speech-writers) *do things with words*: just as much as any poet, they understand that a single choice phrase can work wonders ('we shall fight them on the beaches', 'the lady's not for turning', 'it's the economy, stupid'). As Barack Obama declared in a speech in 2008, echoing such memorable soundbites: 'don't tell me words don't matter – I have a dream'.

Like novelists, politicians make up stories and struggle to keep them coherent. And words, after all, can also be beautiful. Language can sweep you off your feet. Whether it is a poet or a politician, a lawyer or someone wanting to go to bed with you, what is invariably at issue is the *rhetoric of persuasion*. In each case, words do not simply describe but actually do things: they are *performative*. They engage, entice, convince, seduce. Studying literature can immeasurably deepen and enrich our sense of the lying, deceptive, conniving nature of what people or texts say, as well as of how lyrical, lovely and truthful words may be. And sometimes, of course, these tendencies can be very difficult to tell apart. To recall another celebrated proposition from Shakespeare's *As You Like It*, 'the truest poetry is the most feigning' (3.3.16–17).

Of course, the art of persuasion also has to do with what is *not* said. When a McDonald's advert says 'I'm lovin' it', the copywriters don't trouble to explain who that 'I' is, or even what the 'it' is, let alone draw attention to the working conditions of the people who have produced the fast food under consideration or the animals that have died in its cause. (Were they *lovin'* it too?) Studying literature helps us to become alert to the unspoken, unspeakable or unsayable. It enables us to see how far the meaning of a situation, relationship or text is unstated, implicit, doing its work in silence.

Some things are better not said. Literary works can be disturbing because they explore what is transgressive or taboo. Are there limits to such explorations? If so, according to what criteria, on whose authority, in what context? How far can a text go in its depictions of murdering women in contemporary Mexico, for example (in the case of Roberto Bolaño's *2666* (2004)), of combining a confession of serial killing with a zealous love of designer clothing and so-called high-class living (as in the case of Bret Easton Ellis's *American Psycho* (1991)), or of Jenny Hval's celebration of moral chaos and blasphemy in *Girls Against God* (2021)?

Literary studies engages with questions that are at the very forefront of thinking about social and political justice. The very concept of literature is bound up with the democratic principle of 'freedom of expression': that is indeed one of the most fundamental ways in which 'literature' and 'the political sphere' necessarily belong together. As the philosopher Jacques Derrida puts it, the 'institution' of literature allows one to 'say everything, in every way' (Derrida 1992a, 36). In democratic societies, at least, writers are valued for the ways in which they challenge cultural and societal norms and prejudices to make us think differently about our world. Literature has to do with the experience of limits: it probes, delves, tests what is sayable and what it is perhaps not possible to say.

Life and death

Literature is for life. The study of literature deepens and enhances an appreciation of what it is to be alive. D.H. Lawrence famously refers to the novel as 'the bright book of life' (Lawrence 1972, 535), and we hope that everything we say in the present book carries at least a tint of this brightness and speaks to the love of life. Lawrence is on the side of life, rather than any after-life, and he affirms this in ways that can seem unnerving. Much critical and indeed literary writing is tacitly or explicitly respectful of religious beliefs, including the religious belief called agnosticism. Certainly, one might think, there is no harm in being interested in the idea of heaven or paradise. Some poetry and fiction, indeed, is happy to proclaim experiences of the paradisal in the here and now. We might think of the delicious heights of romantic love, as evoked for instance in the words of the Victorian poet and translator Edward Fitzgerald, in quatrain XI of the *Rubáiyát of Omar Khayyám* (1859):

Here with a Loaf of Bread beneath the Bough,
A Flask of Wine, a Book of Verse – and Thou
Beside me singing in the Wilderness –
And Wilderness is Paradise enow.
                                        (Fitzgerald 2009, 21)

Lawrence, however, has no time for such notions. As he puts it in the essay 'Why the Novel Matters': 'Paradise is after life, and I for one am not keen on anything that is after life' (Lawrence 1972, 534).

Literature is also, however, about death. Perhaps more acutely than any other kind of writing, it enables us to apprehend the ways in which life and death are not opposites. Studying literature makes us especially aware of the strange deathliness of writing, starting with the fact that an author's words have a capacity to survive him or her. Most of the literary works that are worth reading are by dead people. Dead people have vast amounts to tell us. There is something ghostly about literary studies, then, and it is not surprising that so many novels, plays and poems have to do with the return of the dead, with haunting or being haunted. Reading involves what the novelist and poet Margaret Atwood calls 'negotiating with the dead' (see Atwood 2002). The literary critic Stephen Greenblatt calls it 'speaking' with them: his book *Shakespearean Negotiations* opens, 'I began with the desire to speak with the dead' (Greenblatt 1988, 1). This is not a matter of the spiritualist or merely fantastical. Rather it has to do with recognizing literature as a great treasure-house of culture, memory and wisdom, not least concerning death, dying and mourning.

Literature and magical thinking

The discipline of literary studies is firmly grounded in reason and in the pursuit of truth. One of the most common misconceptions people have when they first come to study literature at university is to think that they can interpret a literary text in pretty much any way they want. Those suffering from this woefully mistaken idea are often also afflicted by the delusion that all interpretations are equally valid. The study of literature entails the learning and putting into practice of rigorous protocols and methods of reading, critical argumentation and demonstration. This is one of the ways in which, as we will suggest, literary studies is akin to legal studies, and the art of the literary critic closely corresponds with that of the lawyer.

If literary studies is grounded in reason, however, it is also deeply given over to questions of madness and magic, the irrational, uncanny and fantastical. After all, no one can seriously pretend that a novel by Fyodor Dostoevsky, Emily Brontë or Percival Everett, a poem by Emily Dickinson or Gwendolyn Brooks, a play by Samuel Beckett is *reasonable*. Literature is mad. Literature is a discourse in which people say and do crazy things *all the time*. It is not just a matter of there being certain characters who speak or behave in irrational, even psychopathic ways. It is about the very invention or creation of people who are not *real*, of voices that don't exist *anywhere* other than in the realm of the literary work.

This is perhaps especially manifest in a novel or short story because the very structure of such texts involves mind-reading and magical thinking: you encounter a narrator who tells you what other characters are thinking and feeling. But there is a similar dream-like or unreal air to a poem, even if it is a poem about some real event, person or object. In order to make some sense of the literary work, and especially in order to experience what Roland Barthes calls 'the pleasure of the text' (Barthes 1990), you have to submit, at least to some degree, to this madness and magic.

The ordinary and the everyday

At the same time, literary texts also give us the pleasure of the ordinary or everyday, what is *not* (at least not immediately) strange or uncanny or magical or dream-like. Thus Roland Barthes also talks about the pleasure that we take in reading the 'irrelevant' details that novels, in particular, offer, in order to generate what he calls their 'reality effect' (Barthes 1986). A novelist does not *have* to tell you the colour of the wallpaper in a room or the size and shape of a table, s/he does not *have* to describe how the light streams in through the window or how many butterflies are dancing on the flowers outside – the plot will work perfectly well without these 'irrelevant' details. But part of the pleasure of many literary texts lies in the way that they produce the illusion that we are witnesses to a slice of 'real life'. And the details seem to guarantee, precisely on account of their irrelevance to the plot, that this is somehow 'real'. Writers as different as William Wordsworth, George Gissing, Virginia Woolf, Langston Hughes, Ernest Hemingway, Elizabeth Bishop, Raymond Carver, Richard Ford, Zadie Smith and Alice Munro all work hard at times to downplay or sidestep the supernatural, transcendent, ghostly or uncanny in order to focus on the intensity, the fascination and beauty of the ordinary, the everyday, the dull, trivial or banal.

Writers explore the strangeness of the ordinary, its uncanny aspects, it is true. But they also explore the ordinary just because of the wish, indeed the need – which we all at some level have – for the banal, the everyday, the habitual, the familiar. In this way they prompt other kinds of questions in turn: on what basis do we distinguish between the ordinary and extraordinary, the familiar and the strange? Is the sense of 'real life' enough in itself? Why, in this case, do we sometimes prefer to read a work of short fiction, say, rather than watch some so-called 'real life' (a news programme or documentary) on TV? What are 'reality effects' in literature *for*? What is 'real life' exactly anyway?

As the celebrated Russian novelist and lepidopterist Vladimir Nabokov makes clear, both in his novels and in his deceptively autobiographical memoir *Speak, Memory* (1966), we are creatures who indeed enjoy what can variously be called simulacrum, mimicry, realism, virtual reality, mimesis, verisimilitude and accurate or faithful representation. (See the glossary for our explanations of these somewhat technical words.) The ability to copy, mimic, deceive and seduce, as well as to hide, secrete or camouflage, is of course not peculiar to humans (or butterflies) – as Peter Forbes makes clear in his remarkable study *Dazzled and Deceived: Mimicry and Camouflage* (2009). And fooling or pleasing someone with an impression of the real ('That's so life-like!') is not necessarily an innocent or benign activity. 'Fake news' is an obvious and troubling example. The word 'camouflage', after all, is originally concerned with warfare – with concealing camps, guns, ships and so on from the enemy. But there is something remarkable about a story or play or poem that draws us into its world or gives us a new sense of what the so-called ordinary world is like.

Consider the opening lines of a poem such as Wordsworth's 'The Thorn' (1798):

> There is a thorn; it looks so old,
> In truth you'd find it hard to say,
> How it could ever have been young,
> It looks so old and grey.
> (Wordsworth 2010, 24)

Or consider the opening sentences of Ernest Hemingway's novel, *A Farewell to Arms* (1929):

In the late summer of that year we lived in a house in a village that looked across the river and the plain to the mountains. In the bed of the river there were pebbles and boulders, dry and white in the sun, and the water was clear and swiftly moving and blue in the channels. Troops went by the house and down the road and the dust they raised powdered the leaves of the trees.

(Hemingway 2003, 3)

Such openings might readily be compared with the life-like qualities of film or of certain kinds of painting. But there is also a fundamental difference. The poem and the novel are made of language. We can enjoy the 'reality effects' or sense of realism they produce, but they may also prompt us to see something more complex and challenging. They might, in the first place, draw our attention just to the very words out of which the worlds are made – to how strange, for example, that Wordsworthian 'you' (in 'you'd find it hard to say') *is*, since it is not 'you' but the 'I' of the poem that has seen and finds it hard to say anything much about the thorn, or to the way that the apparently literal, prosaic, everyday quality of Hemingway's writing is inflected with figurative and poetic effects (the metaphor of the village that 'looked', the powdering of the leaves, the rhythmical insistence of the word 'and', which appears eight times in this short passage). They might also allow us to see not only that a world such as Wordsworth's or Hemingway's is itself a world of words but also that words in themselves can create or change the world. In this sense, as we will see, there is something radically performative about language – and the study of literature is one of the most instructive and rewarding ways of deepening our understanding of this.

Creative reading

The chapters ahead are informed by a concern with the idea of *creative reading*. Thinking about this idea begins with the realization that reading is not a passive activity, in which you have the words gently wash over you till your eyes reach the bottom of the page before you turn over and set the eyes to re-wash. Reading a good novel or poem or play is like entering a previously unknown country, a love-tangle, a mad-house. And reading also involves writing. To do it well you need to annotate, underline or make notes as you go. To read well is to develop a writing *in response*. To read critically and creatively is to acknowledge and reckon with what the text is saying, with what you (and other critics) think the text is doing or trying to do, and it is also to add something of your own, to bring your own critical and creative concerns to bear on the text that you are reading.

If you fail to annotate as you read, you will forget what it was you found interesting or funny or sad or perplexing, and you won't be able to find those particularly exciting, enticing, intriguing passages or moments again so easily. You may think you will, but you won't. Human memory is weirdly fickle and treacherous. Annotation (including underlining or side-lining) is indispensable. But what do you mark? What is important? What is interesting and what is not interesting? These things vary, even from one reading of a text to the next. And of course you cannot expect to spot every key phrase or moment on a first reading. But you might think to note, for example:

- striking phrases, arresting metaphors, unusual wordings;
- significant events or changes in the direction of the narrative;
- the recurrence of a motif, topic or figure that intrigues you (flowers, say, or telephones, or moments of humour);
- moments of self-reflexivity – moments where a text seems to be refer- ring to itself, for example, where a poem says something about the poem you are reading or about poetry or language more generally;
- significant alterations in narrative perspective (you might, for example, mark places where you feel that the voice of a narrator falters or shifts, perhaps by feigning not to know something or by moving sud- denly into the point of view of one or other of the characters);
- significant alterations in temporal perspective (you might mark a flashback or analepsis, a flashforward or prolepsis, the incursion of a scene of memory or the past in the midst of the present and so on).

Creative reading has to do with ways of reading that are not only rigorous, careful, attentive to historical context, to the specific denotations, connotations and nuances of words and so on, but also inventive, sur- prising, willing to take risks, to be experimental, to deform and trans- form. Creative reading is not about inventing things that are not *in* the text but about inventing new ways of thinking about things that *are* in the text in relation to things *beyond the text*.

Creative reading is careful and attentive to the past, to what other readers and writers have thought, but it is also about the future, about how reading can give rise to new ideas, perspectives and concerns. Creative reading is the key to writing strong, effective and successful literary criticism. In creative reading you might find yourself doing all sorts of unexpected things, including:

- Getting absorbed, even mildly obsessed by the play and meaning of a certain word, phrase, image, figure or idea that would not necessarily occur to other readers: you start tracking it across the text, and this focus on a detail can lead you to a fresh and exciting perspective on the work as a whole.
- Making links between the text you are reading and another text that is by the same author but that is not usually – or perhaps has never previously been – juxtaposed with the primary text (a short story by D.H. Lawrence, for example, might be linked to a letter he wrote years afterwards regarding something ostensibly quite different).
- Making links between the text you are reading and a text by a different author (for example, the way that, from its title onwards, Evelyn Waugh's *A Handful of Dust* evokes T.S. Eliot's *The Waste Land* and the way that the novel responds throughout to the collected works of Charles Dickens).
- Making links between the text you are reading and another, perhaps very different, text or object (a poem by Sylvia Plath, for example, and a science book about the moon or a piece of modern sculpture): the principal challenge here is to ensure that, however perverse they may initially appear, these links are demonstrable, compelling and convincing.
- Seeing a way in which the literary work that you are reading leads to a new, insightful and surprising angle on some pressing aspect of the world beyond the text at hand (justice, the environment, religion and so on).

The term 'creative reading' is hardly recent. As the great essayist Ralph Waldo Emerson noted in 'The American Scholar' in 1837: 'There is . . . creative reading as well as creative writing' (Emerson 1996, 59). Creative reading requires a curiosity about the past, an openness to discovering – with irony or delight – how eloquent, perceptive and thought-provoking writing from earlier centuries or decades can be and how much you thought was new has in fact been (often more eloquently) said or done before. But creative reading can also entail a sense of trepidation and excitement about the future. Reading is an exposure to the unforesee-able. When you are reading a poem, a play, a piece of fiction or even a critical essay for the first time – no matter how 'canonical' it might be, no matter how many thousands of other people have read it and written about it − this reading is something that is happening only to you, with you, at this moment, for the first time in the history of the world. Creative reading is bound up with a critical appreciation of that singularity.

Finally, that singularity, a sense of your unique experience of reading, does not come from the first book (or even the twentieth) that you pick up. Your capacities and skills for creative reading come, slowly but surely, from practice. It is a question of reading carefully, with concentration, imagination and humour, with passion and discrimination, with a pencil at the ready. And beyond all that, the challenge is simply, in the words of Laurence Sterne's *Tristram Shandy* (1759–67), to 'Read, read, read, read, my unlearned reader! read' (Sterne 2003, 203–204). Reading is never the same from one day or even one minute to the next. It can be pleasurable, painful, boring, awe-inspiring. But creative reading is about thinking critically and, at the same time, about tapping into something endlessly and peculiarly promising. It is a matter of trying to make sense of what Emerson means when he says: 'One must be an inventor to read well' (Emerson 1996, 59).

Further reading

There are many books to which you might turn in order to expand and deepen your knowledge of topics and ideas discussed in this chapter. In particular, you might like to look at one or more of the following: the chapter entitled 'Literature' in Bennett and Royle (2023); J. Hillis Miller's *On Literature* (2002); Derek Attridge's *The Singularity of Literature* (2004); Jonathan Bate's *English Literature: A Very Short Introduction* (2010); and Herman Rapaport's *The Literary Theory Toolkit: A Compendium of Concepts and Methods* (2011). For a rich and challenging consideration of many of the concerns touched on in this chapter, see Peter Boxall's *The Prosthetic Imagination: A History of the Novel as Artificial Life* (2020). Mette Høeg, ed., *Literary Theories of Uncertainty* (2021) offers a stimulating collection of essays on literature and the nature of uncertainty. For a rich, entertaining and informative account of rhetorical figures and tropes, see Arthur Quinn's *Figures of Speech: 60 Ways to Turn a Phrase* (2010); an excellent online resource for classical terms of rhetoric is *Silva Rhetoricae* at http://rhetoric.byu.edu/.

Part I
Reading

2. Reading a poem

Reading might seem as easy as A, B, C, or might seem to be something that you do unthinkingly, like breathing or walking or, perhaps, talking. We are bombarded by written messages every day, and those of us who have successfully learnt to read at a young age and who do not suffer from dyslexia or a visual impairment tend hardly to notice the sheer amount of written stuff that we process every waking hour. And the experience of being immersed in or carried away by a book seems to confirm the sense that reading is something that can happen more or less automatically, something that hardly requires thought.

Most of the time, then, reading just happens. You are reading a newspaper, a cereal packet, a road sign, an advertising leaflet, a menu, your mobile phone and scarcely give it a moment's thought. You want the information, and you want it now. But one doesn't read a poem or other literary work just for information. All sorts of other questions come into play as well. You find that you are reading

- for a voice, tone or texture;
- for intriguing effects of language;
- for the way that the writer does things with words;
- for the way that a text seems to foreground the very experience of reading – the question of what reading is and how it works (and perhaps sometimes fails to work);
- for how it baffles or delights;
- for what it is *about* (not always obvious) and what it is trying to do to you, what it prompts or even forces you to think about, even if in spite of yourself.

DOI: 10.4324/9781003301363-3

In what follows, we want to offer some practical tips, as well as to suggest new ways of thinking about the familiar but also oddly unpredictable activity of reading. In particular, we want to explore the idea of 'close reading' – reading, as the nineteenth-century philosopher Friedrich Nietzsche idiosyncratically puts it, 'with delicate eyes and fingers'. In the Preface to his book *Daybreak* (1881), Nietzsche defines the philologist (from the ancient Greek *philo* (love) *logos* (word)). 'Philologist' is another word for 'literary critic', a lover of language and literature, someone concerned to read well: to read well, Nietzsche declares, one should read 'slowly, deeply, looking cautiously before and aft, with reservations, with doors left open, with delicate eyes and fingers' (Nietzsche 1997, 5). Extensive reading, including skim-reading, is an essential dimension of studying literature, and our advice would be to read as much and (when necessary) as fast as possible. But 'close reading', reading carefully, slowly, 'with delicate eyes and fingers', really is what matters. Of course, you might ask how close is close or how slow is slow. As the French mathematician and philosopher Blaise Pascal observes in his *Pensées* (1670), 'When we read too quickly or too slowly we do not understand anything' (Pascal 1995, 16).

You can't win, it seems. So what would it mean to read well, to read closely or to read creatively? In the first place, it means to read with attention not only to what the text says but to *how* it is saying it, to the linguistic and rhetorical features of a work, to its literary 'form', as well as to its sense. It is this double reading or dividing of attention that characterizes literary study. When you read a novel or poem or play, for example, it is all about the way images and ideas are expressed, all about language, about the way words work.

Reading W.H. Auden

We can try to illustrate this by turning to W.H. Auden's poem 'Musée des Beaux Arts' (1939). As its title suggests, this is a poem about a museum. The poem is about looking at pictures and about the relationship between art and suffering.

> About suffering they were never wrong,
> The Old Masters: how well they understood
> Its human position: how it takes place
> While someone else is eating or opening a window or just
>   walking dully along;

How, when the aged are reverently, passionately waiting
For the miraculous birth, there always must be
Children who did not specially want it to happen, skating
On a pond at the edge of the wood:
They never forgot
That even the dreadful martyrdom must run its course
Anyhow in a corner, some untidy spot
Where the dogs go on with their doggy life and the torturer's
    horse
Scratches its innocent behind on a tree.
In Brueghel's *Icarus*, for instance: how everything turns away
Quite leisurely from the disaster; the ploughman may
Have heard the splash, the forsaken cry,
But for him it was not an important failure; the sun shone
As it had to on the white legs disappearing into the green
Water; and the expensive delicate ship that must have seen
Something amazing, a boy falling out of the sky,
Had somewhere to get to and sailed calmly on.

                                        (Auden 1979, 79–80)

   The language of Auden's poem seems very straightforward, indeed
almost *un*-poetical. The poem does not include many of the kinds of
metaphors, specialized or 'poetic' diction, regular rhythm and other
rhetorical effects that one tends to associate with poetry. Although the
word-order is inverted in lines 1–2 ('The Old Masters were never wrong
about suffering' would be more usual in everyday speech), you could
almost mistake the poem for a version of someone speaking, informally
commenting on some paintings in a museum.

   Look, for example, at the way that the subject of the poem, 'The Old
Masters', is introduced as if as an afterthought, parenthetically, in line 2;
or at the way that the extended fourth line strolls rather casually, even
quite dully, from one everyday action to another ('eating or opening
a window or just walking dully along'). Like much modernist verse,
the poem strives for a certain ordinariness or 'naturalness' of language,
evoking everyday speech patterns while being, at the same time, highly
crafted. And perhaps that is no surprise: after all, the poem is itself *about*
ordinariness, about the way that life just carries on, even if a calamitous
or momentous or amazing event is occurring nearby.

   You can get a sense of this odd combination of the ordinary and the
amazing by looking at how the rhymes work. Although it is easy to
miss, the poem does mostly rhyme: in fact, only line 3 is unrhymed (no

word rhymes with 'place'). But the rhyme-scheme is so complex and irregular that you could easily overlook it. The rhyme-scheme of the first section runs: abcadedbfgfge (where the 'a'-rhyme is 'wrong' / 'along', the 'b'-rhyme 'understood' / 'would' and so on). Through its rhymes, the text both acknowledges and conceals its specialness. The poem does rhyme, but irregularly (line 1 rhymes with line 4, but line 2 has to wait until line 8 for its rhyme and so on).

We might also note the easy, apparently casual rhythm of the language and the variation in stressed and unstressed rhyme-words. Crucial to all these effects is the marvellously quirky enjambment – lines that end without punctuation or pause, where the sense runs on ('how it takes place / While . . .'). Along with their casualness, there is an artfulness about the line-endings that ramifies the hazards and coincidences of life that the poem is contemplating. Part of Auden's achievement in constructing this poem, in other words, has to do with the intricate and subtle ways in which he exploits the sound-effects of verse to suggest that things are a matter at once of chance and device, that the world and the poem are at once poetic and prosaic – both amazing and unremarkable. And that is what the poem is about: paying attention – finding things remarkable or not.

Poems and paintings

Auden's poem is in the venerable tradition of 'ekphrastic' poems – poems that try to evoke paintings, sculptures or other visual works. ('Ekphrasis' is a technical word that originates in the Greek for 'description' and is used for the attempt by a work in one medium to represent a work in another.) The poem asserts that the 'Old Masters' alert us to something important about humanity – that a momentous event for one individual (birth, for example, or death) may not be of much consequence to unrelated bystanders. Something remarkable, tragic, appalling happens to someone, while for others in the vicinity life just goes on, unperturbed.

But how does painting, or art more generally, relate to this? In the first section of the poem, the speaker describes two unnamed (and perhaps fictitious) paintings from the Musées Royaux des Beaux-Arts in Brussels, one of which seems to depict the birth of Christ (the 'miraculous birth') and the other his crucifixion (the 'dreadful martyrdom'). The speaker is struck by the way that these world-changing events happen against the background of children blithely skating, dogs doing what dogs do and the torturer's horse being more concerned with an itch on its backside

Figure 2.1 Pieter Brueghel (c.1527–69), *Landscape with the Fall of Icarus* (1569): the legs of Icarus can be seen disappearing into the water in the bottom right-hand corner of the picture.

than about what its master might be up to. These animals and children don't care, and why should they?

The second part of the poem more specifically concerns a painting in the same museum thought to be by the sixteenth-century Dutch painter Pieter Brueghel (c.1527–69), entitled *Landscape with the Fall of Icarus* (1569). The painting depicts the death of the mythological figure of Icarus, whose father, Daedalus, had made his son wings of feathers bound together with wax. Although his father had warned him not to fly too near the sun for fear that the wax would melt, Icarus does so and, his wings disintegrating, falls into the sea. In Auden's poem, the speaker comments on the way that in Brueghel's painting a ship sails 'calmly on', ignoring this momentous event (momentous for Icarus, since he dies, but not of much consequence to anyone else, it seems).

As critics have pointed out, one of the interesting dimensions of Auden's poem is that, unlike the Old Masters, the speaker is wrong – wrong in particular about the Old Masters (see Heffernan 2004, 147). While Brueghel's painting does indeed build on Ovid's account in the *Metamorphoses*, Book 8, to highlight the way in which the death of Icarus has minimal impact on the rest of the world, there are plenty of paintings by Old Masters in which suffering *is* put centre stage and made the focus of general attention.

You might think, for example, about the way that the Spanish painter Francisco Goya (1746–1828) is explicitly concerned with what it means to suffer, with the horrors of the brutality of war, and with what it means to come across or to be a spectator at another's suffering. There is no sense that anyone is looking away from the suffering individuals in his 'Disasters of War' series (1810–20), paintings in which the combination of inhuman brutality and human suffering is the central and even sole topic.

Reading elegy

Auden's poem also intersects with other traditions. In particular, it is possible to link 'Musée des Beaux Arts' with the tradition of elegy. There is a moment in the Mike Newell film *Four Weddings and a Funeral* (1994) when John Hannah, playing Matthew, recites another famous Auden poem, 'Stop all the clocks' (a.k.a. 'Funeral Blues') (1936). The poem figures mourning as the impotent desire for the whole world to stop because the person one loves has died. 'Stop all the clocks, cut off the telephone, / Prevent the dog from barking with a juicy bone', the poem begins, 'Silence the pianos and with muffled drum / Bring out the coffin, let the mourners come' (Auden 1979, 141).

This is no doubt an experience many of us have shared and will share – the sense of being appalled that the world simply goes on regardless when someone close to you has died. 'What is wrong with people that they can just go on with their ordinary, unremarkable lives, in the face of this catastrophe?', we might find ourselves wondering, in incredulity. And this indeed is one of the foci of the elegiac tradition – the tradition of poems of mourning. Because his friend and fellow poet Edward King has died, Milton argues, even nature itself is in mourning: 'thee the woods, and desert caves, / With wild thyme and the gadding vine o'ergrown, / And all their echoes mourn' ('Lycidas' (1638), lines 39–41 in Milton 2003, 40). In 'Adonais' (1821), Shelley's speaker laments the fact that his grief 'returns with the revolving year' even while 'The amorous birds now pair in every brake' and while 'A quickening life from the Earth's heart has burst / As it has ever done' ('Adonais', lines155, 159, 164–165, in Shelley 1977, 396). In a more domestic vein, Alfred Tennyson asks in *In Memoriam* (1850) 'How dare we keep our Christmas-eve[?]', when he has 'such compelling cause to grieve' the death of his friend Arthur Henry Hallam (section 29 in Tennyson 1989, 372).

The tradition of remarking on the disjunction between our own grief and the insouciance of others, even of nature, is also alluded to in Derek Walcott's sequence of elegies for his mother in his 1997 collection *The Bounty*. There is 'the traffic of insects going to work anyway' – anyway, despite his mother's death – and there is a sense of 'astonishment' even 'that earth rejoices / in the middle of our agony' (Walcott 1997, 3, 14). And there is also something perhaps still harder to bear: our tendency to forget our grief just as and even just because we try to memorialize it in a formal elegy: 'pardon me', Walcott demands plaintively and self-reflexively, 'as I watch these lines grow and the art of poetry harden me // into sorrow as measured as this' (5).

The desire to stop all the clocks can also be a form of narcissism, a troubled realization that the world does not revolve around your existence and therefore around your grief or suffering. So 'Musée des Beaux Arts' connects with 'Funeral Blues' and with the elegiac tradition more generally by highlighting and putting into question a narcissistic fantasy about being at the centre of the world, about the desire for the world to take note, to notice you. In 'Musée des Beaux Arts', the speaker's (erroneous) idea about the profundity of the Old Masters' understanding of the human predicament, their understanding, always, that human suffering goes unnoticed, can then be seen as part of a concern about being and not being noticed.

This is a way of reading 'Musée des Beaux Arts': we have begun to try to tease out the thematic core of the poem, the poem's 'message' (as it is sometimes crassly called), or its 'theme', what it 'says' or what it is about, and we have remarked on its links with other poems in the elegiac and ekphrastic traditions. And we might join other critics in linking the poem to its historical contexts. A number of critics have suggested that the ignored or disregarded suffering that Auden alludes to in his poem includes the Spanish Civil War, for example, in which he had been personally involved, as well as the rise of Hitler in the 1930s, and other events of what, in his poem '1 September 1939', he calls that 'low dishonest decade' (see Cheeke 2008, 107–108).

Considering the question of its historical resonance is one way to pursue a close and creative reading of Auden's poem. The poem is about the nature of examples, but it is more than merely an example. It points beyond itself. Indeed we could say that one of the most forceful underlying arguments of the poem is that it is always necessary to take context into account but that context is always larger and more complex than the point of view of any single individual.

Reading and paraphrase

There is a famous essay by the 'New Critic' Cleanth Brooks called 'The Heresy of Paraphrase' (Brooks 1949), in which Brooks argues powerfully and influentially that a poem should not be understood to have a propositional content in the way that, say, this sentence or a newspaper story does. As Archibald MacLeish famously puts it at the end of his 'Ars Poetica' (1926), 'A poem should not mean / But be' – although as MacLeish also rather less famously says in that poem, 'A poem should be wordless / As the flight of birds' (MacLeish 1963, 50–51), which does rather make you wonder how seriously to take it (for the record, 'Ars Poetica' contains 129 words).

Brooks argues that to try to extract the content or meaning from a poem, to attempt simply to paraphrase it, is a kind of 'heresy', a fundamental error, since it is in the very nature of literary texts that *what* they say is bound up with *how* they say it. After all, like translation, strictly speaking, paraphrase impossible. You cannot paraphrase without altering. As Bill Readings memorably puts it, 'paraphrase is a philosophical joke'

(Readings 1991, xxi). And even if you could do it, *just* paraphrasing anyway would not get you very far. Paraphrase may be helpful, even necessary, but a reading of a literary text should start rather than stop there.

We have talked about the language and rhetorical structures of Auden's poem, about its linguistic plainness or 'naturalness' – with respect to the syntax and lexical details in particular – and about the way it rhymes but at the same time seems to resist regular and overt rhyming. This is the fundamental premise of close reading: vocabulary, syntax and rhetorical effects cannot be distinguished from a poem's meaning. The rhyme-scheme will tell us very little unless we can link that feature persuasively to a consideration of other aspects of what the poem is doing and above all to how it makes meaning. What Auden's poem means has to do with the way that the casualness of the apparently un-poetic voice interacts with the poem's veiled poeticalness.

Poetry and truth

We have suggested that the speaker is wrong to declare that the Old Masters have only one approach to suffering. In the real world, so to speak, and especially if the speaker was, say, an art critic, that error would be a problem. When art critics make generalizations about paintings or about the Old Masters, they are supposed to get their facts right, or at least to speak with veracity – that, after all, is their job. But when poets make demonstrably false propositional statements, the erroneousness of their assertions only serves to complicate and enrich the experience of reading. Poems and other literary texts do not, in a sense, make propositional truth claims – or if they do, those claims should themselves be understood as rhetorical tropes.

To put it bluntly, it doesn't *matter* whether or not the claim the speaker makes is true, any more than it matters whether Jane Austen's famous generalization at the beginning of *Pride and Prejudice* (1813) ('It is a truth universally acknowledged, that a single man in possession of a good fortune, must be in want of a wife') is true (Austen 2006a, 3). Her statement is effective precisely to the extent that it is questionable (particularly as a truth *universally* acknowledged): until Austen wrote this sentence one might think that the sentiment was anything but 'universally acknowledged'. It was perhaps more generally acknowledged afterwards, at least among a certain social class, by certain heterosexual men and women, in a certain historical period. And in that sense, the sentence is 'performative': it performs or produces what it presents itself as only describing. But we are still perhaps enticed and indeed even charmed by the grand, if somewhat complacent authority of the narrator's voice. What Austen is doing at the beginning of her novel is not so much expressing a universal truth as establishing for her narrator a certain voice or claim to authority.

Questions of the poem

Like Austen's opening, Auden's generalization about the Old Masters provokes a series of questions that are fundamental to reading:

- First, there are questions of voice and authorship: Who is speaking? To what extent are these views the poet's own? Whose voice is this? In what tone or tones are we invited to hear it?
- Second, there are the questions of sincerity and intentionality: Does the speaker mean what he says? Does Auden? What does Auden want to convey?
- Third, there is irony: Should we be alert for the distinction between what is said and what is meant? In other words, does the poem say one thing and mean another?
- Fourth, there is form and content: How do technical factors such as the rhyming, alliteration, enjambment and so on participate in the sense?
- And finally, there is interpretation: How should we construe this poem's sentences? How can we ensure that our reading is accurate, valid, credible?

Careful attention to these questions, and especially to distinctions such as those between poet and speaker or author and persona, is fundamental to effective critical reading.

So we are left with a poem that makes a bold, assertive statement but that is also *about* the act of making bold assertive statements, a poem that raises questions (about voice and intention and meaning and irony and so on) without necessarily resolving them. Indeed, what we have is a sense of tension or paradox or uncertainty with regard to the poem's meaning or its meaningfulness. The poem seems to be utterly lucid, transparent, interpretatively straightforward. But that very simplicity generates hermeneutic or interpretative problems.

There is a fundamental strangeness about the way in which the poem moves between the particular and the general. We need to respond to the ways in which the poem is general (it is about poetry, painting, suffering and so on). And at the same time we need to acknowledge its particularity or singularity. We need to try to do justice to the ways in which 'Musée des Beaux Arts' is untranslatable, unparaphrasable.

The relationship between the general and the singular was noted by Aristotle in his *Poetics* more than two thousand years ago. But it is a principle that has been reinvented, rediscovered, restated in different ways down the centuries – most recently, for example, by W.K. Wimsatt (1954, 69–84) and Jacques Derrida (1995a, 142–143). Briefly, in the *Poetics* Chapter Nine, Aristotle argues that unlike history, which seeks to record and account for single, individual and essentially unrepeatable events, but also unlike philosophy, which is based on the establishment of universal truths without regard for the singularity of the event, poetry is about *both* the particular or individual or singular *and* the general or universal (Aristotle 2001, 97–98).

In this context we might notice, then, the rather strange ways in which Auden's poem involves both very large generalizations (about *all* the Old Masters being right about something *all* of the time) and three very specific examples. What happens in 'Museé des Beaux Arts' is that a general statement is made and then exemplified. But in exemplifying the statement, the speaker seems to get caught up, lost even, in the detail, in the particularities of the paintings, and especially with respect to Brueghel's painting of the fall of Icarus. We might thus notice, for example, the particularity and queer eroticism of the boy's white legs in the corner of Brueghel's picture as they disappear into the sea.

And this, in a sense, is what happens to us – or what could or should or might happen to us – in reading Auden's poem. Although we start out wondering what it means, what argument or ideas are being conveyed, we quickly get drawn in by the verbal and rhetorical effects, by the language, in short by *how* something is being said rather than simply *what* is being said. We might think here about anaphora, the rhetorical figure for the repetition of a word or phrase at the beginning of successive lines or clauses. Once you have noticed it, for example, it is difficult to ignore how insistently the poem speaks of 'how': 'how well they understood', 'how it takes place', 'How when the aged . . .', 'Anyhow in a corner', 'how everything turns away'.

This brings us to our final point about reading a poem. People, including many critics and theorists, often seem to assume that there is a clear and final distinction between the *practice* of reading, close reading in particular, and literary *theory*. Indeed, people often seem to suppose that there is a sense in which close reading and literary theory are mutually exclusive: you can't read closely, carefully, slowly if you are also doing theory, they say; theorizing about literature is obstructed or distorted by reading, by attending to the idiosyncrasies of individual texts, they think. But this overlooks the fact of literature's singularity, its strange mixing of the general and particular. Close reading is necessarily bound up with questions of theory – and theory itself is always a question of reading. As soon as you begin to ask questions about a poem ('What does it mean?', 'What kind of text is it?', 'Was the author male or female?' and so on), you are engaging with theoretical questions and issues.

Summary

Here, in summary, are some fundamental points about how to read poems and about how to read them *well*:

- **Paraphrase**, if you like: it can be helpful. But recognize that a paraphrase is never an end in itself. Saying that Auden's 'Musée des Beaux Arts' is about suffering is just a beginning.
- **Attend** to *how* a poem says something as well as to *what* it says. Look, for example, at how the intricacies of the rhyme-scheme in Auden's poem help to propound its meanings.
- **Think** about how the language and rhetorical effects reflect or enact, enhance or nuance a poem's meaning. The plainness, the un-remarkableness of Auden's language reflects his subject, the way that ordinary, everyday life just goes on, oblivious to extraordinary events.
- **Be sensitive** to issues of authorial intention that your reading brings up and be ready to engage with these as integral to the poem's meaning and significance. Is Auden being ironic, oblique, understated, misleading, playful? What are his intentions here? What weight should we anyway give to authorial intention?
- **Be alert** to allusion. How does Auden's poem interact with 'Funeral Blues' and other poems? In what ways does the poem engage with, revise, respond to the ekphrastic tradition of poems on paintings? What is distinctive or singular about *this* poem's painterly qualities?

- **Respond** to the ways that a poem is itself, in a self-reflexive way, attentive to the question of reading. In Auden's poem, looking at pictures might be taken to be a form of reading, and the poem might be understood to be about what Frank Kermode, in a book of that name, calls 'Forms of Attention' (Kermode 1985).

- **Consider** how the poem moves between the particular and the general. Auden's poem is in part *about* the way that one generalizes from particular examples, but it is also *about* what is stubbornly singular in the particular.

- **Tease out** the logic of the poem and try above all to explore what is conflictual or paradoxical or ironic. Auden's poem is about paying attention and not paying attention to amazing events, and is itself both amazing and very ordinary – giving the sense that the ordinary may itself *be* extraordinary, and may even be more interesting, in some ways, than what seems extraordinary.

- **Remember** history: in what ways is this poem embroiled in the historical, cultural, social and economic as well as perhaps personal circumstances in which it was written and published? As we indicated earlier, critics have suggested that Auden's poem should be read in contexts including the Spanish Civil War and the rise of Nazism in the 1930s. History cannot explain *everything* about a poem, but it does help us to better understand crucial features.

- **Examine** details: get stuck on words, images, rhetorical figures, formal features such as rhyme and rhythm. What is the word 'human', for example, doing in line 3 of Auden's poem? What is its relationship to the dogs and to the torturer's horse later on, and to the non-human ship which is nevertheless anthropomorphized by being given the human attribute of not noticing or stopping to help when it 'sees' Icarus fall to his death? What does the poem tell us about what it means to be 'human'? Well, that might be the beginning of another reading of the poem. Perhaps we should start again . . .

- **Note**: the singularity of the poem is something that calls for a singular response to it in turn. Can you make a note of something surprising or striking that this poem does to you? Is there a way in which you can integrate this sense into your account of the poem? Reading well, or creatively, entails not just noticing what other readers might be expected to notice but also adding something of your own – taking a path or flight across the poem that involves new connections, new resonances, new possibilities.

Further reading

You are spoilt for choice when it comes to introductions to poetry, most of which pay careful attention to its formal aspects. You might try Michael D. Hurley and Michael O'Neill's brief, lucid and carefully focused *Poetic Form: An Introduction* (2012), or rather more expansive books such as John Strachan and Richard Terry, *Poetry* (2nd edn, 2011); Tom Furniss and Michael Bath, *Reading Poetry: An Introduction* (2022); and John Lennard, *The Poetry Handbook* (2005). Three brief, readable, thought-provoking and sometimes intentionally provocative books on poetry (as a way of writing and as texts to be read) by practising poets are David Constantine's *Poetry* (2013), Glyn Maxwell's *On Poetry* (2012) and James Fenton's *An Introduction to English Poetry* (2003). William Empson's amazing *Seven Types of Ambiguity* is now almost a hundred years old, but it set high standards for close reading when it was published in 1930 and still constitutes a remarkable demonstration of just how close you can get to 'the words on the page'. Ekphrasis (and specifically poems about paintings) is a very lively area of literary studies: see, in particular, Stephen Cheeke's *Writing for Art: The Aesthetics of Ekphrasis* (2008); James A.W. Heffernan's *The Poetics of Ekphrasis from Homer to Ashbery* (2004); and three brilliant books by W.J.T. Mitchell: *What Do Pictures Want?: The Lives and Loves of Images* (2005), *Picture Theory: Essays on Verbal and Visual Representation* (1994) and *Iconology: Image, Text, Ideology* (1986). Specifically on the question or problem of paraphrase, it is worth looking at Cleanth Brooks's classic essay 'The Heresy of Paraphrase' (1949). Finally of general and illuminating interest, see Derek Attridge and Henry Staten, *The Craft of Poetry: Dialogues on Minimal Interpretation* (2015), and Lucy Newlyn's playful but instructive guide, *The Craft of Poetry: A Primer in Verse* (2021).

3.   Reading a novel

People often talk about being 'lost in a book'. Perhaps you have experienced this yourself. Enthralled by the textual drama being played out in your head, you forget the weather, the time, your surroundings, who you are with − even who you are. You forget these things and, for the time of that forgetting at least, don't really care.

There is a wonderful moment in Elizabeth Bowen's 1963 novel *The Little Girls* that evokes this sense of being lost in a book but evokes it from the outside, so to speak. One of the eponymous little girls, Clare, occupies herself with a puzzle in the sitting room of her friend's house, while her friend's mother reads a book:

> The scarlet, brand-new novel, held up, masked its wholly-commanded reader's face. Though nominally she was 'lying' on the sofa, the upper part of the body of Mrs Piggott was all but vertical, thanks to cushions − her attitude being one of startled attention, sustained rapture and, in a way, devotion to duty. . . . She was oblivious of all parts of her person as she was of herself. As for her surroundings, they were nowhere. Feverel Cottage, the sofa, the time of day not merely did not exist for Mrs Piggott, they did *not* exist. This gave Clare, as part of them, an annihilated feeling. She burned with envy of anything's having the power to make *this* happen. Oh to be as destructive as a story!
>
> (Bowen 1964, 78)

Clare is piqued, troubled by the fact that she has become nothing in the face of this book. She wishes she had such power, and she feels, in the face of it, 'annihilated'. It is possible to get carried away by other art forms, to be sure − to be swept up breathless into the energies and

DOI: 10.4324/9781003301363-4

excitement of a film, to be powerfully moved by a piece of music, to be held rapt by a picture or to be engrossed in a play. But there is something unique, something very particular, about being lost in a novel, an experience that can go on all day or for day after day in the case of a really long novel. And it is something that happens inside your head in a way that makes it both convivial and reclusive at the same time. Novel reading is the most social of activities (you are getting inside other people's heads when you read novels, and they are getting inside yours) and one of the most anti-social activities in the world (reading is a mostly solitary, silent activity, effectively subverting any idea of community or communitarian ideal).

The history of the novel

The novel in its modern form is a strange creature, a peculiar cross-breed or chimera. It emerged more than three hundred years ago out of various forms of storytelling and *reportage* – journalism, the epistolary (letter-writing), accounts of remarkable lives, chronicles, travellers' tales, romances, ballads, news-sheets and so on. Partly for this reason, the novel is almost infinitely malleable: it is highly diverse in its form, in its subject-matter and in its style.

Constantly evolving, then, the novel adheres to no consistent set of rules or procedures. One might say that the rule of the novel is to break the rules. In fact, the novel is always – how can we put it? – *novel*. The word 'novel' comes from the French *nouvelle*, which originates in the Latin *novellae*, meaning 'news'. So one way of thinking of the novel might be as a narrative that tells us something 'new' – it reads you the news, so to speak. Certainly, novels that work well are those that give you a sense that you are experiencing something new. They tell you a story, present you with people, places, situations, events, ideas and feelings in a way that seems new, fresh, even unprecedented. That, in a word, is what a novel is, or should be: it records, explores and prompts you to think of something new, in a new way.

Saying that the novel is novel amounts to little more than a tautology. How might we define it? It is not easy. But the *Oxford English Dictionary* has a go. Citing examples of the word from the mid-seventeenth century onwards, the dictionary explains that a 'novel' in the modern sense is a 'long fictional prose narrative', that it usually fills 'one or more volumes' and that it 'typically' presents 'character and action' with 'some degree of realism and complexity' (*OED*, novel, n. 4b).

The last point is curious: novels, we are told, are 'realistic', have 'some degree of realism'. What does *that* mean? After all, novels are generally classified as 'fiction' – certainly that is how bookshops and libraries group such works. The word 'fiction' also includes the short story and novella, of course, but is in any case taken to designate the kind of writing that *departs* from the real, from what we like to think of as real life. Fiction is, after all, thought of as precisely *not* 'real' life, not true. In fact the novel is shot through, from its beginnings in the late seventeenth century right up to today, with this question of its fictional / real status. In a sense, that is what every novel entails: an experience of undecidability, uncertainty about the real.

Why does the *OED* insist on this element of so-called 'realism'? Novels typically give us the sense that they are describing the 'real' world, or that they are describing what the real world could be like, or creating something that might be a world, an alternative world, one that looks and feels something like our own, ordinary, everyday, 'real' world. There are plenty of novels, and indeed whole genres, that depart from this sense of the real – science fiction, fantasy novels, magic realism, for example. But such novels are almost always underpinned by a recognizable if distorted sense of the familiar world (by the laws of physics, for example, or by conventional ideas about character or time or causality). The power and strangeness of Aldous Huxley's dystopian novel *Brave New World* (1932), for instance, depends on the ways in which we compare the brave newness of its imagined world with the old and familiar.

What we must never forget, however, is that 'realist' and 'realistic' are never simply the same as 'real'. Indeed, as the critic Pam Morris bluntly comments of realist novels: they '*never* give us life or a slice of life, nor do they reflect reality' (Morris 2003, 4). This might seem para-doxical, given the name 'realism', but the point is that it is a *convention* of representation: realist fiction follows certain conventions in describing the world. After all, a novel is made of words; it is not a mirror. As the Marxist critic Pierre Macherey argues, the novel is 'analogous to' (rather than a representation or version of) 'reality': 'the imaginary universe is not a reflection of the real universe', he goes on, since it constitutes a 'system of reality' such that the 'project of writing a novel' is 'inevitably remote' from 'that of telling the truth' (Macherey 2006, 299). Indeed, these notions of the conventionality of realism have a troubling corol-lary: perhaps the sense of the 'real' that novels purport simply to present is in fact a way of *constructing* reality for us. Perhaps it is, at least in part, precisely by reading narratives such as novels that we invent for ourselves a sense of what the 'real' world is like.

Some examples might help. The journalist, merchant, political pamphleteer and life-long debtor Daniel Defoe (c.1660–1731) also produced some of the earliest novels in English. His two most famous, *Robinson Crusoe* (1719) and *Moll Flanders* (1722), present fictional but credible accounts of relatively ordinary people in relatively extraordinary situations.

Robinson Crusoe recounts Crusoe's attempt to survive on an island on which he is stranded after a shipwreck. The novel is based on the model of contemporary travellers' tales (which, like all travellers' tales every-where, no doubt, were themselves embellished, improved, exaggerated or simply false), as well as on an account of Alexander Selkirk's actual experience of being a castaway between 1704 and 1709. Defoe allows his readers to imagine such a situation through the vivid detailing of the objects, events and people that his hero encounters. The full, rather lengthy title-page to the first edition of the novel that is now known as *Robinson Crusoe* gives no indication that the events described did not happen. Indeed, in its excessive detailing of events and in its witholding of Defoe's name, it goes to considerable lengths to suggest that they *did* actually happen (see Figure 3.1).

Paratexts

The title-page of a novel is a paratext. Other paratexts include prefaces, notes, introductions and so on. This title-page suggests that the adventures to which it alludes really occurred, 'strange' and 'surprizing' as they may be. Although these events did not happen, Defoe works hard to persuade us here that they did. The narrative is to be 'strange' and 'surprizing' because it is new, but it is nevertheless familiar, true-to-life, realistic.

Defoe's scandalous fictitious 'life' of Moll Flanders is similarly devoted to propounding a sense of the 'real', of historical authenticity. The novel that we now know as *Moll Flanders* is presented as a memoir written by the character herself (see Figure 3.2). In tabloid-headline style, the title-page entices readers to buy the book by mentioning the major events in the scandalous life of Moll Flanders. The book is presented not as a novel but as a version of Moll's own 'memorandums', as if it were simply a transcription of her personal diary. The life of the rather ordinary Moll Flanders is extraordinary, 'surprizing', like Crusoe's, and, like Crusoe's, her narrative is presented in such a way as to allow Defoe's

Figure 3.1 Title-page to Daniel Defoe, *Robinson Crusoe*, first edition (London, 1719).

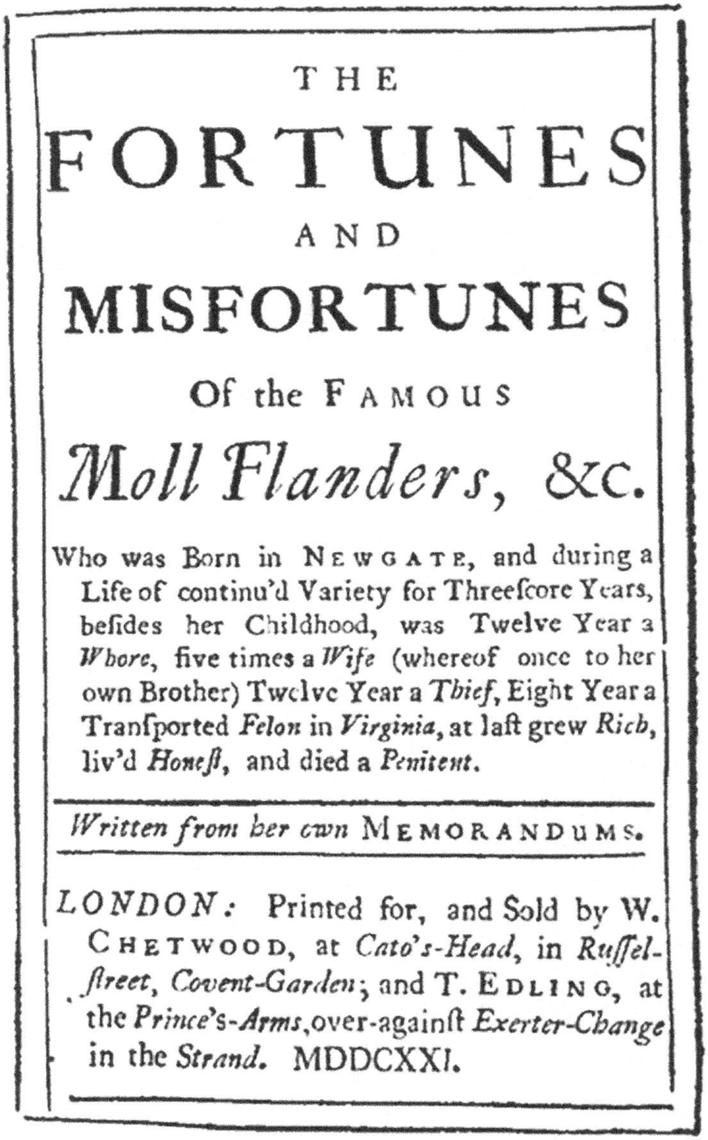

THE

FORTUNES

AND

MISFORTUNES

Of the FAMOUS

Moll Flanders, &c.

Who was Born in NEWGATE, and during a Life of continu'd Variety for Threescore Years, besides her Childhood, was Twelve Year a *Whore*, five times a *Wife* (whereof once to her own Brother) Twelve Year a *Thief*, Eight Year a Transported *Felon* in *Virginia*, at last grew *Rich*, liv'd *Honest*, and died a *Penitent*.

Written from her own MEMORANDUMS.

LONDON: Printed for, and Sold by W. CHETWOOD, at *Cato's-Head*, in *Russel-street*, *Covent-Garden*; and T. EDLING, at the *Prince's-Arms*, over-against *Exerter-Change* in the *Strand*. MDDCXXI.

Figure 3.2 Title-page to Daniel Defoe, *Moll Flanders*, first edition (London, 1721 [1722]).

contemporaries to suppose that it is a faithful record of actual historical events. These are not fictions, the title-pages suggest, and they are not written by a novelist.

What both of these title-pages insist on is the historical *authenticity* of the narrative to be recounted. In this respect they would appear to be indistinguishable from a later work that is considered to have an entirely different referential status, the remarkable *Narrative of the Life of Frederick Douglass, An American Slave, Written by Himself* (1845). The development of the novel indeed is characterized by a concern with the relationship between historical authenticity and invention or fiction. So while contemporary novelists may not explicitly claim that their narratives are historical accounts or concern actual events, they tend nevertheless to work hard to produce *effects* of credibility, of 'reality'. Contemporary fiction is often portrayed as preoccupied, even obsessed, with the relationship between its own fictionality, its inventedness and the real that it purports to represent. In fact, however, this has been the condition of novel-writing from the beginning.

Realism and interiority

Kazuo Ishiguro's compelling novel *Never Let Me Go* (2005) exemplifies this concern to construct a sense of a real place, a real world, and to play on the expectations that that sense of the real produces in the reader. The first part of the novel is set in Hailsham, a fictional but seemingly stereotypical boarding school of the late twentieth century. There is one crucial difference from your average boarding school, however: the reader is gradually made aware that the children in this school are clones and that as adults they will effectively be farmed for their body-parts, which they will 'donate' to 'normals' (non-clones, people created by conventional means).

Ishiguro's novel is highly 'realistic' in the sense that the descriptions of people, places and events are credible and indeed largely accord with the conventions of boarding school narratives from Thomas Hughes's *Tom Brown's School Days* (1857) to Anthony Buckeridge's *Jennings* books (1950–94) to J.K. Rowling's *Harry Potter* books (1997–2007). But at the same time, Ishiguro has invented a parallel world in which some individuals are classified as not human and are, as young adults, slowly killed in order to provide body-parts for others, those classified as human. The novel asks fundamental questions about what it means to be human, what it means to treat others as objects. *Never Let Me Go* works hard to convince us that a world that does not exist in fact does, or could do. Part of the pleasure that we take in reading this and other novels has to do with an experience of uncertainty, a delicate balancing of verisimilitude with a sense of the impossible.

So a sense of realism – what eighteenth-century critics (following Aristotle) called 'probability' – is an integral dimension of the novel. It is precisely this creation of the probable, the elaboration of a world in which we can believe, that allows us to get imaginatively lost. But in addition to this sense of realism and to the other elements that the *OED* identifies – character, action, complexity – there is another important feature of the novel that the dictionary overlooks, namely the way it allows us unprecedented access into the minds of its characters. While lyric poems give readers a sense of what one person – the poet or speaker – is thinking, they do not typically present the interiority of a *series* of other people. And while plays usually present the actions of a number of individuals, they are not very good at presenting interiority.

Interiority in plays tends to be presented, rather awkwardly, in the convention of the soliloquy, a convention in which the character talks to him- or herself out loud, so that s/he may be overheard by the audience (although curiously not by any other character who might happen to be on the stage). Shakespeare's Iago, for example, talks to himself with dazzling eloquence as he wonders about how to bring about the downfall of the noble Othello, before concluding: 'I haven't, it is engendered! Hell and night / Must bring this monstrous birth to the world's light' (*Othello*, 1.3.402–3). Dramatic soliloquy (literally 'speaking alone') is an oddly artificial convention and usually only takes up a small proportion of a character's time on stage. And yet it is a crucial historical antecedent for the novel. The figures of Iago, Hamlet and Macbeth, for example, thinking aloud on stage, anticipate and inspire the interiority of characterization that we associate with the modern novel. Nonetheless, it is in the novel that you can get inside other people's heads most comprehensively, most intimately. This is the 'special life-likeness' of the novel, as one critic puts it, and it depends paradoxically but crucially on 'what writers and readers know least in life: how another mind thinks' (Cohn 1978, 5).

A sharing of interiority is crucial to how we get lost in the 'world' of a book. We come to inhabit other minds and bodies imaginatively, becoming other to ourselves. This process of empathizing or identifying is not restricted to novels, of course. Human beings spend enormous amounts of time trying to work out what other people are thinking and feeling and desiring and imagining and believing. In particular, they spend a lot of time thinking about what others are thinking about them.

What you want to know – what you *need* to know – is what other people are thinking, and especially what other people are thinking about you.

Mind reading

Novels are the great art form of mind-reading. Indeed, we would argue that they reflect on other minds in richer and more nuanced ways than any other discourse, including psychiatry, psychology and psychoanalysis. Novels allow us to know, or perhaps more accurately to imagine or believe that we know, precisely what goes on in the minds of others, to understand other minds. So in reading, discussing, studying and writing about a novel, it is important to consider how it presents other minds, how it creates and plays with this illusion.

The novels of Jane Austen (1775–1817) are intently alert to all these issues. Austen takes as her subject a certain class of people – the middle- and upper-middle classes living in southern England around the beginning of the nineteenth century – and pays scrupulous attention to their manners and relationships, their opinions, prejudices and ways of speaking, their lifestyles and purchasing preferences, their habits, occupations and finances. And their love lives. *Especially* their love lives. The typical Austen heroine is middle-class but financially insecure, young, unmarried but eminently marriageable and dependent on finding a husband for a resolution to her life.

What Jane Austen realized is that there is nothing more important in these women's lives than the ability to read the minds of others. She recognized that the happiness of these young women, if not their very existence, depended on this skill, and that no minds needed to be read with more care than those of these women's suitors, their potential husbands. Given the constraints of social discourse and the lack of available information, Austen's young heroines have to make high-risk decisions about the honesty, integrity and trustworthiness of the men who come into their orbit by effectively reading their minds.

Austen's novels can be seen as mind-reading training manuals. She is dealing with a particular socio-economic predicament, one that requires a particularly skilful decoding of the lives of others. And it is, we suggest, for this thematic reason that Austen's novels are so technically accomplished: theme (what the novels are about) and technique (how they work) come together in the way that these novels present other minds. Austen's heroines are by necessity professional mind-readers – in a sense, mind-reading is their *only* profession.

In this way they are in collusion with the Austenian narrator, who is the presiding expert at the subtle and complex construal of others' minds. And just as the society that Austen depicts requires people to say things by not saying them, and for characters to surmise what is not said, she is herself accomplished at saying things by withholding them, by indirection. This occurs most pervasively by means of irony, by saying one thing and meaning another. In this respect, Austen makes us, novel readers, mind-readers too. We are, in effect, compelled to read the narrator's mind.

Here, by way of example, is a brief passage from the opening pages of Austen's final novel, the posthumously published *Persuasion* (1818). The passage concerns the views of the snobbish and self-regarding father of the novel's heroine Anne, the widower Sir Walter Elliot:

> For one daughter, his eldest, he would really have given up any thing, which he had not been very much tempted to do. Elizabeth had succeeded, at sixteen, to all that was possible, of her mother's rights and consequence; and being very handsome, and very like himself, her influence had always been great, and they had gone on together most happily. His two other children were of very inferior value. Mary had acquired a little artificial importance, by becoming Mrs. Charles Musgrove; but Anne, with an elegance of mind and a sweetness of character, which must have placed her high with any people of real understanding, was nobody with either father or sister: her word had no weight; her convenience was always to give way; – she was only Anne.
>
> (Austen 2006b, 6)

The questions of who is speaking and whose views are being expressed call for careful analysis. We need to try to figure out exactly what the narrator is trying to convey, what she means, to work out what she is thinking: we need to read her mind. But this is not as simple as it might seem, since the narrator is not presenting a pure, unmixed version of her own thoughts or opinions but instead mixing them up with those of her characters, in particular with those of Sir Walter Elliot. Because at this point, Austen is trying to convey several different concerns: she is trying to give us a sense of a) what Sir Walter thinks, so that we can get a sense of b) what his financially dependent daughter Anne is up against and, relatedly, c) what the narrator thinks of what Sir Walter thinks.

This last point is decisive. Novels do not only give us a sense of their characters' minds, but allow us – require us, indeed – to understand what the narrator might be thinking. In the striking statement that 'His two other children were of very inferior value', for example, we have to wonder who is speaking, and who thinks this. This is a 'third person' narrative in which the narrator does not appear explicitly as a character. She is 'omniscient' (or, more accurately perhaps, 'telepathic') in the sense that she seems not only to know about everything that happens but also to be able to tap into what different characters are thinking and feeling.

No doubt it is the narrator who says 'His two other children were of very inferior value'. But to whom do these children seem of 'inferior value'? Is this the perspective of the narrator? To talk about someone as of 'very inferior value' involves a distinctive and disturbing set of assumptions – the assumption that a person has objectively measurable 'value', that some individuals are 'inferior', while others are presumably highly superior and so on. The sentence seems to take a chillingly instrumentalist stance on a person. And since it refers to Anne, the heroine of Austen's novel, who is otherwise presented as flawed but admirable, we must conclude that the views expressed by these words, and even the words 'inferior' and 'value' themselves, are not the narrator's so much as those of the snobbish and thoughtless father.

So through an apparently objective, omniscient or telepathic third-person narrator, Austen is in fact presenting the assumptions and prejudices of one of the characters, Sir Walter Elliot. We are reading Sir Walter's mind, in other words, getting an insight into what he thinks. But we are also implicitly and perhaps more importantly getting an insight into what the *narrator* thinks of what Sir Walter thinks. We thus infer that she does not think much of Sir Walter's brutal, instrumentalist, class-ridden opinion of his daughter's value. It is this *critique* of Sir Walter's prejudices that the passage may be said finally to convey in this indirect, wonderfully ironic way.

The technical term for the narrative technique whereby the narrator moves freely and flexibly from her own perspective into and out of the minds of her characters is 'free indirect speech' or 'free indirect discourse'. Jane Austen was one of the first to develop this technique – a technique that is still pervasive in the novel today.

From third-person to first-person narrative

Free indirect discourse is a feature of third-person narratives. But mind-reading also occurs in relation to first-person narrators. Paradoxically, first-person narrators often know themselves less well than we know them. And it is this gap of insight, of self-knowledge, that first-person novels most richly explore and exploit. To illustrate this we could return to the case of Ishiguro's *Never Let Me Go*. As she begins her story, the thirty-one-year-old narrator Kathy H. proudly boasts of her abilities as a 'carer'. She has spent more than eleven years caring for other clones as they 'donate' their body-parts and eventually die. She has apparently been told that she has eight more months to go before she will end her time as a carer and become a 'donor' herself. Ishiguro manages to generate enormous pathos by making us see the limitations of Kathy's sense of her own humanity – her inability to think beyond the terms of a world in which she has been sentenced to a painful, selfless death. She is not trying to boast, she tells us:

> But then I do know for a fact they've been pleased with my work, and by and large, I have too. My donors have always tended to do much better than expected. Their recovery times have been impressive, and hardly any of them have been classified as 'agitated', even before fourth donation. Okay, maybe I *am* boasting now. But it means a lot to me, being able to do my work well, especially that bit about my donors staying 'calm'. I've developed a kind of instinct around donors, I know when to hang around and comfort them, when to leave them to themselves; when to listen to everything they have to say, and when just to shrug and tell them to snap out of it.
>
> (Ishiguro 2005, 3)

Ishiguro deftly maps the limits of his narrator's understanding. Kathy H. is what is known as an 'unreliable narrator'. Ordinarily, an unreliable narrator fails to tell the truth, or obfuscates, or misleads. Kathy does none of these things – at least not on purpose. Rather, she remains enigmatic to us: she is unreliable because she is unable to fully appreciate the true ethical and existential horror of her own situation. Her proud boast about her ability to keep her donors calm is, as we will later learn, grounded in the appalling, agonizing early deaths that she has overseen and that she will soon herself suffer at first hand.

Ishiguro's dystopian vision of England, then, presents a world in which certain individuals are treated as if they are not human. But what is striking and moving about Ishiguro's prose is the fact that Kathy H. is unable quite to grasp something fundamental that her readers do understand: everything she says, all her pride and compassion, all her humanity, indeed, is undermined by a gaping hole in her ethical understanding, by her inability to see that her society treats her inexcusably, inhumanly. Ishiguro generates immense pathos through this technique of narratorial blindness. Kathy H. is blind to the full horror of the story she is narrating. Everything comes through the voice or perspective of an individual who cannot see the enormity of the crimes committed against her and those like her.

Ishiguro's novel is perhaps a more sophisticated example of a book that carries us away, in which we can get 'lost'. It creates a parallel world in which we can believe, inventing characters with whom we can identify, and at the same time it resists such identification, prevents us from fully losing ourselves. The novel brings us up short. In a subtle and intricate way, Ishiguro produces what the German poet and playwright Bertolt Brecht refers to as the 'alienation effect' (Brecht 1964, 136–147), inasmuch as his novel refuses to offer us the easy comfort of identification with his novel's narrator and protagonist, Kathy H.

All of the novels we have discussed in this chapter – *Robinson Crusoe*, *Moll Flanders*, *Persuasion* and *Never Let Me Go* – have been turned into TV or cinema films in recent years. Despite their best efforts, however, movies make a massive loss in translating written texts onto the screen. They lose the voice and the consciousness of the narrator, the personality, the texture of the minds of others. It is such voices that echo in our heads as we read these novels, and such presences that reverberate.

Like the artifice of soliloquy in plays, the convention of the voice-over is occasionally employed in movies to mimic the novelistic narrator. But this tends to feel un-filmic, and is usually dropped fairly quickly, while other cinematic aspects – scene, spectacle, sound, music, dialogue, action – take its place. Only in novels do we get these particular kinds of voices, the thoughts and feelings of others inhabiting our heads. Only in novels do we get this verbal richness that allows us, as the novelist David Foster Wallace puts it, to 'leap over the walls of self' (Wallace 1998, 51). Only in novels do people inhabit our thoughts in this way, prompting us to reflect on the idea that they read our minds as we are reading theirs.

Questions for the novel

How should you examine a novel? The following are some questions for you to think about:

- What work is the title doing? Are there other paratextual features of the book that are of interest (a preface or notes or introduction or acknowledgements and so on)?

- In what ways does the novel examine, play with, subvert or in other ways explore the relationship between language and representation (or text and world)?
- What other texts does the novel evoke, develop, ironize, challenge? What genres does it engage or identify with, mimic, satirize or deviate from?
- How are characters represented and developed? What kinds of language and rhetorical effects are used to describe them? What is individual or idiomatic about the way in which a particular character speaks?
- What kind of narrator is employed? Is it first-person or third-person? How much does the narrator seem to know? Is s/he omniscient, telepathic, unreliable? Ironic? Playful? Is s/he a character in his or her own right? Is there more than one? How does the narrator interact (if at all) with the characters and with the reader?
- How is the narrative focalized (through whose eyes are the events seen and understood)? Whose language and perspective does the narrator use to describe events, characters, objects, scenes?
- What kinds of lacunae are involved in the narrator's perspective? What does s/he *fail* to understand or perceive? Does s/he withhold information? How (and how do you know)? Why?
- How do concerns with racism, misogyny, class and the environment, relate to the concepts and ideas we have discussed in this chapter?
- And finally, what does the novel do with the uncanny, humour, shock, dream, sadness, terror, love, eroticism, ghosts, God, the future, wordplay?

Further reading

The eminently readable title essay in David Lodge's *Consciousness and the Novel* (2002) is good on the ways that novels seem to allow us access to other minds, while Dorrit Cohn presents a more technical and more detailed consideration of the novelistic presentation of consciousness in her book *Transparent Minds* (1978). A valuable recent development of these ideas of novelistic discourse is Timothy Bewes's *Free Indirect: The Novel in a Postfictional Age* (2022). Probably the most influential book on the early development of the English novel is Ian Watt's Marxist analysis in *The Rise of the Novel* (1957), which connects it with the socio-economic rise of the middle classes and the ideology of possessive individualism in the late seventeenth and eighteenth centuries. Two important revisions to Watt's narrative were published in the 1980s: Lennard Davis, *Factual Fictions* (1983) and Michael McKeon, *The Origins of the English Novel* (1987). Robert Caserio and Clement Hawes, eds., *The Cambridge History of the English Novel* (2012) traces the development of the novel (in Great Britain, as well as in Ireland and the Caribbean) from its earliest times to the late-twentieth century. Another classic study of the novel that we would recommend is the shrewd and pleasingly anti-authoritarian *Aspects of the Novel* (1927) by E.M. Forster. Brian Richardson's *Unnatural Voices: Extreme Narration in Modern and Contemporary Fiction* (2006) offers a valuable overview of subsequent developments in novelistic practice. In *Studying the Novel* (2022), Jeremy Hawthorn offers a brief but comprehensive survey of many of the topics that we touch on in this chapter. For an important corrective to the often rather loose usage of the term 'omniscient narrator', see Chapter 8 in Jonathan Culler's *The Literary in Theory* (2007).

4.   Reading a short story

How short is a short story? What does 'short' mean in this context? One critic is brave, or foolhardy, enough to proffer some numbers, stating that a prose narrative of anything up to about fifty pages (say 20,000 words) can be classified as a short story. A prose narrative of more than about 150 pages (50,000 words or so) is then classed as a novel, while between the two there is that half-way house, the novella – texts such as Herman Melville's *Billy Budd* (1886–91) or Joseph Conrad's *Heart of Darkness* (1899), George Orwell's *Animal Farm* (1945) Claire Keegan, *Foster* (2010), or Natasha Brown, *Assembly* (2021) (see Scofield 2006, 4–5). In a famous discussion of the short story published in 1842, one of the great early masters of the form, Edgar Allan Poe, argues that the fact that a story takes between half an hour and two hours to read allows for a 'unity' of form: 'During the hour of perusal the soul of the reader is at the writer's control', he claims. There is no 'weariness', he says, no need for interruption: everything comes at one sitting. The short story produces what Poe calls 'a single effect' (Poe 1965, 106–108).

To be brief, then. That is the thing. As Adrian Hunter suggests, the short story involves 'the art of saying less but meaning more' (Hunter 2007, 2). In the Introduction to his *Collected Stories*, the short story writer V.S. Pritchett argues that the short story is concerned with 'concision, intensity, reducing possible novels to essentials'. He comments that the short story writer is 'a mixture of reporter, aphoristic wit, moralist and poet' (Pritchett 1982, x–xi). A typical short story lacks formal chapters, requires a relatively simple plot-line with little in the way of sub-plot, and attempts little in terms of character development. It relies on 'poetic tautness and clarity', according to Elizabeth Bowen, another

DOI: 10.4324/9781003301363-5

great exponent of the form, and it 'stand[s] on the edge of prose'. It is, she says, 'nearer to drama than to the novel' (Bowen 1950, 38).

The present

On the face of it, then, there is not much to the short story – so how do we read one?

Closely related to Poe's notion of 'single effect', short stories often turn on a single event, or, more particularly, on a moment of recognition or awakening. James Joyce famously referred to such moments as 'epiphanies', borrowing this term from the Christian idea of a 'manifestation' or 'showing forth' in which Jesus Christ is revealed to the Magi. Joyce's secular epiphany retains a sense of the interaction of the natural with the supernatural. In *Stephen Hero* (written c.1904–6), Joyce defines 'epiphany' as 'a sudden spiritual manifestation' constituting 'the most delicate and evanescent of moments' (Joyce 1963, 211).

Short fiction often revolves around a moment of recognition or revelation, but the epiphany is not necessarily religious or even illuminating. It might be a moment of opacity or uncertainty, of obscurity or indecision. Another helpful approach to short fiction is to consider such a work as an elaboration on a single sentence, or phrase, or word. Indeed, relying on what has been called 'elliptical suggestiveness' (Malcolm and Malcolm 2008, 7), many short stories can be considered elaborations on their own titles.

There is a remarkable, disturbing work of short fiction by the American writer David Foster Wallace called 'Suicide as a Sort of Present' (1999) that brings out these ideas about titles and epiphanies particularly well. Wallace's work hinges on the question of how we interpret its opaque but also intriguing and provocative title. What does it mean to call suicide 'a sort of present'?

Uncertainty here revolves around the meaning of the word 'Present'. 'Present' can denote a gift or it can mean something that is here, now. Since the idea that suicide might be a *gift* of some sort appears to be aberrant, if not abhorrent, 'Present' in the title seems at first glance to mean 'now' or 'here'. But this is odd as well: how can suicide be here or now? And why only 'sort of'? Is there some obscure philosophical idea at work here? By the end of the narrative, however, the problem appears to be resolved: it is evident that 'present' does indeed mean 'gift'. In this regard, the whole point of the story comes down to the question of how suicide can possibly be conceived of as a gift, even a 'sort of' gift. On one level, at least, the story and its title function as a kind of riddle.

How does Wallace work this conundrum? The story involves a mother who has 'a very hard time indeed, emotionally, inside' (Wallace 2000, 241). She is a high-achieving perfectionist whose failure to live up to her own standards leads to self-loathing: 'Her expectations of herself were of utter perfection, and each time she fell short of perfection she was filled with an unbearable plunging despair that threatened to shatter her like a cheap mirror' (241–242). Her desire for perfection is transferred onto her son, who naturally fails to live up to his mother's 'impossibly high' expectations (242). The high standards that the mother expects of herself require that she loves her son unconditionally. And her perfectionism also means that she detests his failings: 'every time the child was rude, greedy, foul, dense, selfish, cruel, disobedient, lazy, foolish, wilful, or childish, the mother's deepest and most natural inclination was to loathe it' (243).

But there is a disconcerting twist to the mother's predicament: since a 'good mother' cannot loathe her child, instead of loathing him for these failings, she loves him more, because not to do so would be to fail as a mother. Indeed, paradoxically, the *more* loathsome the child is, 'the more loving the mother required herself to be' (Wallace 2000, 243). And she turns her loathing inward and loathes herself even more for the loathing she feels for his failings. Because the son loves his mother more than anything else in the world he therefore paradoxically fails more in order to gain more of her love – since the worse he behaves the more, perversely, she loves him. The only way out of this double bind of love and loathing is, as we discover when we reach the final paragraph, for the son to kill himself. The story doesn't actually say that he kills himself, it is true – instead it tells us that because the mother is unable to express her feelings of love and loathing, the son, who is 'desperate, as are all children, to repay the perfect love we may expect only of mothers', finally 'expressed it all for her' (244).

Putting this sentence together with the story's title and with a reference in the final paragraph to the boy becoming old enough to 'apply for various licences and permits', we can infer that the son's 'present', his 'gift', is to buy a gun and shoot himself, thereby, within the terms of his own perverse and paradoxical psycho-logic, producing the perfect 'expression' of his mother's conflicted feelings of love, loathing and self-loathing. It is in this way that the title's conundrum, the idea that suicide can be a 'sort of present', is resolved.

Wallace's really quite disturbing and even misogynistic text is none-theless, in other respects, characteristic of the short story more gener-ally. It has a single and relatively simple plot. It contains a small number of characters whose development is limited. It concludes in a kind of epiphany whereby the title's word 'present' is resolved as 'gift'. It is all there in the single resonant, ominous phrase, '[he] expressed it all for her'. This is a story about loathing and self-loathing, and about mater-nity and a child's psychological development – a story about the way that a mother' hands on misery' to her son, as Philip Larkin might have put it (see 'This be the Verse' (1971); Larkin 2012, 88). And it is tightly focused on that one titular word and its implications: 'present'.

Works of short fiction also tend to be concerned with the present in the other, temporal sense, with a sense of 'now', of immediacy, of presence. Nadine Gordimer contends that short story writers 'see by the light of the flash': their art is 'the art of the only thing one can be sure of – the present moment'. In the short story, events are presented 'without explanation of what went before and what happens beyond this point', she claims (quoted in Hunter 2007, 2). Gordimer seems to be pointing to something important in the form. The 'flash' has been variously described, in fact. Pritchett observes that the short story is 'the glancing form of fiction' (Pritchett 1982, xi).

Wallace talks in an interview about stories coming together with 'the click of a well-made box' (Wallace 2012, 35). He borrows this idea from a letter by W.B. Yeats on the idea of a poem coming 'right with a click like a closing box' (Yeats 1940, 24). In the same interview, Wallace refers to James Joyce's notion of 'epiphany', linking stories with a form of spir-itual manifestation or revelation. In Joyce, however, and in Wallace and others, this 'click' or flash or epiphany is *both* revelatory and obscuring – mysterious or unfathomable, uncanny. Indeed, it might be said that what distinguishes such authors from hack writers is the difference between a 'twist in the tale' that reveals everything, that leaves no more to be said or imagined, and the kind of 'click' or 'flash' or epiphany that at once closes and opens up the text to further reading and thinking.

There is much more we might say about Wallace's story. We could explore at length the rich verbal texture of the narrative, the way that, for example, in the form of something like a psychological case-study, it satirizes therapeutic discourses. Thus, so-called 'therapy-speak' – as a child, the mother was seen as 'bright, attractive, popular, impressive' (242) but, as an adult, her self-loathing 'tended to project itself outward and down-ward onto the child' (242) and so on – gets incorporated into the casual

discourse of contemporary American conversation. We read that she has
'a very hard time of it, emotionally, inside' (241); that, as a child, she had
'some very heavy psychic shit laid on her' by her parents (241) and so on.
We could also talk about the way that Wallace produces a searing analysis
of the social and psychological, the political and institutional discourses of
late twentieth-century America, the way that this intricately psychological
tale also involves a deeply felt critique of the social and cultural institutions
(including the 'institutions' of the family and of education) that nourish
such agonizing, pointless, deadly self-loathing in the first place.

A good story

Let us consider another example. In Flannery O'Connor's story 'A Good
Man is Hard to Find' (1953), the wording of the title again proves crucial.
The title sounds like a quotation, and a quick internet search reveals that
the phrase originates in a 1918 song of the same name by Eddie Green,
made famous in the following decades by Bessie Smith, Sophie Tucker
(the original 'Last of the Red Hot Mamas') and others. But Flannery
O'Connor's writings tend to have prominent religious dimensions, and
this story proves to be no exception. The title, we quickly discover, also
has a Biblical resonance. The idea of a good man being hard to find
occurs in Mark 10:18 when Christ refutes the claim that he is himself a
'good man', commenting that 'There is no man good, but one, that is
God' (see Desmond 2004, 129). And in fact the same phrase is used in
an even more apocalyptic line in Micah, one of the books of the Old
Testament: 'The good man is perished out of the earth: and there is none
upright among men: they all live in wait for blood'. 'Trust ye not in a
friend', Micah continues, ominously (Micah 7:2, 5).

   O'Connor's 'Good Man', then, involves a number of allusions. But
where does knowing this get us? Recalling or researching individual
words and phrases is all very well and it is fine to speculate on where a
phrase in a story originates, but we need to go further. Allusion-spotting
is akin to that oddly inconsequential hobby, train-spotting. Like train-
spotting, it is basically harmless. But neither, in truth, gets you very far.

   So how do these allusions *work* in O'Connor's title? Perhaps the point
is that it is not just *hard* but in fact *impossible* to find a 'Good Man'.
Eddie Green's second line tells us that 'You *always* get the other kind';
Micah's apocalyptic worldview encompasses only violence and distrust
('there is *none* upright among men'); and Christ denies that *any* man,
whether or not he is the son of God, can be described as 'Good'. These

sentiments seem to chime with O'Connor's work: her fictional world is characterized by alienation and disillusionment, mental and physical disability, random acts of violence and cruelty, deception, unkindness, in short the elusiveness of moral and spiritual 'goodness'.

O'Connor's 'A Good Man is Hard to Find' concerns a family from the deep South: husband and wife, two children, a baby and the man's mother. The father, Bailey, wants to take the family south to Florida for a holiday, but his mother wants to go north to Tennessee. As part of her case against travelling south, she cites news reports of a violent escaped convict self-dubbed 'The Misfit' who is said to be heading for Florida. Florida is a dangerous place to visit, she argues, and Bailey is acting irresponsibly in taking his family there. But Bailey ignores his mother's advice and the family set off in their car. In a farcically random accident on the way, Bailey crashes the car into a ditch. Another car comes by with three men in it. Unfortunately, Bailey's mother recognizes one of them as the Misfit, and says as much. His response is darkly menacing:

> 'Yes'm,' the man said, smiling slightly as if he were pleased in spite of himself to be known, 'but it would have been better for all of you, lady, if you hadn't of reckernized me.'
>
> (O'Connor 2009, 127)

Since he has been 'reckernized' and identified as the escaped convict, the Misfit tells the two other men to take Bailey and his son to the nearby woods: 'The boys want to ast you something', he says politely but ominously to Bailey, 'would you mind stepping back in them woods there with them?' (128). Soon two gun shots are heard and the men return without Bailey or his son. Next, Bailey's wife, daughter and baby are taken to the woods and with a kind of gruesome inevitability a scream and three pistol shots are heard. While all this is happening, the grandmother engages the philosophically minded but psychotic Misfit in an ethico-religious discussion, in which she attempts to persuade him that he is really, at heart, a 'good man'. She tells the Misfit that she knows he has 'good blood' and urges him to pray, but to no avail: as she reaches out to touch him, the Misfit shoots her dead (O'Connor 2009, 131–132).

The narrative relies for much of its dark humour, lambent pathos and sharp, almost nihilistic sociological critique on the stark evocation of the linguistic registers of the American South – of Bailey, the grandmother, the children, the Misfit and of the owner of a roadside diner where the family stop to eat before the car crash. In particular, there is a focus on

the title-word 'Good'. When the family stop at the diner, the grandmother engages in a conversation with the owner, Red Sammy ('Red',
we might surmise, because he expresses left-wing views). Micah-like, they
talk about the recent decline of society and of manners, and she agrees
with Red Sammy that nobody is to be trusted 'these days'. Red Sammy
tells her that he recently allowed a customer to take some gas for his car
on credit and asks why she thinks he did such a naively trusting thing:
'Because you're a good man!', declares the grandmother, before under-
mining her argument by saying that there 'isn't a soul in this green world
of God's that you can trust' while looking directly at Red Sammy. Red
Sammy replies that 'A good man is hard to find' (O'Connor 2009, 122).

Part of the force of Red Sammy's comment involves the fact that
he is not saying anything new or necessarily sincere, that he is quoting
from or at least echoing a pop-song or half-remembered phrase in the
Bible. He seems to be spouting a cliché. It is only later, when the grandmother engages the Misfit in conversation as he calmly has his men shoot
each member of her family in turn, that this tired cliché returns with
despairing force. 'I know you're a good man', the grandmother tells him
with increasing desperation, 'I know you're a good man at heart . . .
I just know you're a good man' (127–28). But the Misfit disagrees after
pondering her proposition a while: 'Now, I ain't a good man', he says
after a darkly comic pause, 'but I ain't the worst in the world neither'
(O'Connor 2009, 128).

It is debatable, of course, whether the Misfit is the worst in the world,
but as he himself affirms, he is certainly not 'good'. And yet O'Connor
is evidently rather taken by the Misfit's eerily psychotic way of thinking
about morality, about what it means to be 'good'. His way of thinking
about ethics and about punishment includes the idea that it doesn't matter
what you do because you will be punished anyway, even if you don't
know or have forgotten what it is that you have done to deserve the punishment, and that he can never 'fit' what he has done or not done with the
punishments he has been made to endure (hence the Misfit's name). For
him, Jesus threw 'everything off balance' by raising the dead and thereby
forcing us to choose whether to believe in him (according to which
reasoning, we should logically abandon everything else and follow him)
or not believe in him (in which case, following strict logic, we are free to
do anything, to take our pleasure where we will) (O'Connor 2009, 131).

After shooting the grandmother dead, the Misfit offers the reader
a final insight into his home-made and ethically bizarre sense of what
'good' means: challenging even linguistic sense, he declares that the

grandmother 'would of been a good woman . . . if it had been some-body to shoot her every moment of her life' (O'Connor 2009, 133). The Misfit's deformations of grammar ('would of been'; 'if it had been somebody') seem to reflect the deformations in his ethics. In a sense, the statement eludes both meaning and logic. O'Connor's disturbing but also disturbingly funny ending brilliantly evokes the impossibility and vio-lence of both saying and doing what the Misfit wants to say and would do.

'Good', then, does an enormous amount of work and the play on the word is integral to what make it a *good* story. O'Connor explores the ethical, theological, criminological, psychiatric, political and socio-logical dimensions of the word. She evokes the idea of the 'good' in an uncanny, surprising and unsettling way – in a way that is really only avail-able in fiction, and with a concision and intensity that is characteristic of short fiction at its most powerful. She re-invigorates the tired, seem-ingly banal word 'good' in prose that evinces 'tautness and clarity', while hovering at the same time on the edge of sense. By putting pressure on the word 'good' and the idea of a 'good man' in this way, O'Connor's story investigates the limits of morality, religion and sense itself.

Summary

Here is a summary of the points we have tried to emphasize in this chapter:

- **Think small**: the short story's brevity has particular consequences for its form. Often allusive and elliptical rather than discursive in manner, short stories tend to focus on a small number of characters and are often based on a single incident. They often involve a sense of epiphany or revelation even as they complicate any sense of reso-lution or closure.
- **Begin with the title**, or at least come back to it at the end: what does it tell us? How does it work? In what ways does the story elab-orate on, depart from, resolve or even resist its own title?
- **Be suggestible**: if short fiction involves 'elliptical suggestiveness' then it is important to pay careful attention to nuances of phrasing and word choice. What kinds of denotations, implications, associ-ations and connections are produced by and through individual words and phrases in the story? Attend to what Bowen calls the 'poetic' – effects of syntactical deformation, unusual metaphor, striking turns of phrase, arresting images.

- **Look out for repetition**: there are often key words or phrases that recur or seem to stand out in a short story. A single word (like 'good' in O'Connor's story) can often provide a way into thinking and writing about the story.

- **Talk about the plot**: when writing about a work of short fiction, it is often helpful to summarize the plot (as we have done in the case of the two stories we consider in this chapter). It is always instructive and often surprising. It is a way of finding out what you think, what matters to you in the story under consideration. The way that you retell the plot is never innocent or neutral: you are inevitably being selective and partial, and thus, in effect, already foregrounding a particular reading.

- **Be alert to effects of intertextuality**: look for ways that the story seems to be alluding to, echoing or explicitly referring to stories, poems, songs or other kinds of text. How do these echoes, allusions, references function? How do they enrich or complicate the text? What are their effects?

- **Ask yourself**: What is the most striking, memorable or significant aspect of this story? Your answer may have to do with its overall impact on you, its 'single effect' as Poe called it, or it may have to do with something much more peripheral or micrological (a particularly powerful image or situation or idea or word or phrase, for example). Either way, you should think about a way of incorporating this, when writing about the story.

- **What is the time?** Or, in more precise terms, what is the temporal perspective of the story? Does it locate itself historically, for example? Is the narrator looking back on something that happened long before, or very recently? (It may even be that the story is being narrated in the present tense.) How much time is covered in the course of the narrative? In what ways does the story play with time – dealing, for example, with events over many months or years in a single paragraph, but elsewhere devoting an extended passage to what happens one afternoon or even at one moment?

- **Who's talking?** Consider the importance of the figure of the narrator, narrative voice and narrative perspective. Is this a third-, first- or even second-person narrative? Is it omniscient, telepathic, unreliable, involved, detached and so on? And what about dialogue in the story? In what ways do verbal exchanges between characters deepen our sense of them as characters, but also contribute to the action and atmosphere of the story?

Further reading

Two good places to start for general overviews of the short story tradition and of how short stories work are Andrew Kahn's *The Short Story: A Very Short Introduction* (2021), and Adrian Hunter's *The Cambridge Introduction to the Short Story in English* (2007). In Paul March-Russell's wide-ranging *The Short Story: An Introduction* (2012), the short story is taken as an essentially fragmentary form that has had a significant impact on the development of literature more generally. It is also worth looking at Frank O'Connor's now-classic book on the topic *The Lonely Voice: A Study of the Short Story* (1963). We also recommend Anne-Marie Einhaus, ed., *The Cambridge Companion to the English Short Story* (2016) for a helpful general overview of the genre. Some of the most influential studies of the short story have been written by practitioners themselves. An excellent anthology of such material is Charles E. May's *The New Short Story Theories* (1994). Since in the English-speaking world, the American short story is arguably the most sophisticated and well-developed tradition, Martin Scofield's *The Cambridge Introduction to the American Short Story* (2006) is also very helpful. For studies of the British and Irish short story, see Cheryl Alexander Malcolm and David Malcolm, eds., *A Companion to the British and Irish Short Story* (2008); Heather Ingman, *A History of the Irish Short Story* (2009); and Andrew Maunder et al., *The British Short Story* (2011).

5. Reading a play

How can you read a play? What sort of question is that? What sense does it make to talk about *reading* in the context of a play? Surely you go to a play to watch and listen, not *read*? We will attempt to explore these questions in relation to one of the most famous plays of all time, Shakespeare's *Romeo and Juliet* (first published in 1597). But before we do so, a brief prologue is called for.

Prologue to reading Shakespeare

To study a play by Shakespeare is inevitably to find yourself turning for help to other sources. You shouldn't feel bad about this. Everyone does it – from actors and theatre directors to Shakespeare editors and other scholars. Glosses and editorial commentary, online or other 'study guides' that offer you information about character, plot and theme, the setting of the play, its performance history and its publishing history – all of these are helpful. An edition of the play that provides detailed commentary and notes is a must: the Arden, the New Cambridge and the Oxford World's Classics Shakespeare editions are all excellent in this regard. (In the following pages we will rely on the Oxford edition of *Romeo and Juliet*: see Shakespeare 2000.) If you can, we recommend seeing a performance of the play. A play is for watching (and listening to) – its happening on the stage is decisive – even if, as we hope to show in this chapter, it also has a separate and compelling existence on the page.

So much of a play by Shakespeare (or indeed by anyone else) will become suddenly much clearer when you actually see it being acted. A live performance has a special immediacy and vitality, but there are

DOI: 10.4324/9781003301363-6

also some great film versions. We would suggest that, in the first instance, you avoid contemporary remakes or other modern dramatizations. Film versions of *Romeo and Juliet* by Franco Zeffirelli (1968) or Baz Luhmann (1996) are brilliant in all sorts of ways but take you quite a long way from the play Shakespeare wrote. It is easy enough to get hold of the BBC version with Patrick Ryecart, Rebecca Saire, John Gielgud and others (1978, dir. Alvin Rakoff), for example, in order to see a performance that is more faithful to the text.

Watching a performance of *Romeo and Juliet* encourages you to think about how the script is being interpreted, about what the director and actors are doing with it. This involves numerous aspects that are not necessarily specified in the text (or in the stage directions) and that require intelligence and imagination on the part of the theatre group staging the event. These include:

1. **Location**. The play is set in Verona, but every scene entails different questions about exactly how and where − a street? A bedroom? A banqueting hall? A graveyard?
2. **Time**. The play would appear to take place in the late-medieval period, although it also has obvious hallmarks of the more contemporary, that is, English Elizabethan.
3. **Facial gestures and other movements of the body**. The performance will raise questions of how actors move and speak or remain silent, how they interact with one another and with the audience.
4. **The physical space between characters on the stage**. Sometimes they are as far apart as possible, sometimes unnervingly close, literally nose to nose or lips upon lips.
5. **The use of props**. Stage furniture can take on a life of its own − a balcony, a bed, a tomb, as well as smaller objects such as a sword or shield, a letter or phial of poison.

It is probably only after you have watched a production that sticks quite closely to Shakespeare's text that you can start working out what to make of the play. This is because part of the pleasure of reading a play by Shakespeare is in imagining it being staged.

Imagine yourself as the director *and* as the actor in question. When Juliet exclaims, 'O Romeo, Romeo, wherefore art thou Romeo? / Deny thy father and refuse thy name', and Romeo responds in an aside (i.e. talking to himself) 'Shall I hear more, or shall I speak at this?'

(2.1.76–80), there are countless ways of delivering these lines. Imagine how you would speak them, in the moonlit beauty of this so-called balcony scene. No one is asking you to be a director at the Old Vic or at Stratford or a glamorous and dazzling actor on the stage. Your vision of how the scene is staged and acted may be thoroughly derivative: it might correspond very closely to the way in which you remember it being performed on stage. But still, that playing of the lines, in the private theatre of your head, is a crucial prologue to *writing* about the play.

A good critical essay about *Romeo and Juliet* will convey a strong sense of how the play works – what the characters are like, how the plot unfolds and other aspects of play-making and play-production that we have mentioned. Above all, it should convey knowledge and curiosity about Shakespeare's language. The best critical writing invariably provides in-depth commentary on one or more passages from the play, showing how this fits in with the play's larger concerns. Curiosity and patience are often as important as knowledge and self-assurance. So much of the richness of Shakespeare's language depends on what is ambiguous or uncertain. With Shakespeare, perhaps more than with any other writer in English, it is often as important to acknowledge uncertainty, as it is to demonstrate knowledge. It is important, as John Keats comments, to 'remain in uncertainties, Mysteries, doubts' (Keats 2005, 60). This is what Keats calls 'negative capability', a quality that he considers profoundly Shakespearean.

But how do you read a play? This, in a sense, is a question the play itself asks. For as we will see, *Romeo and Juliet* is very much a play about reading – and about failing or being unable to read.

To the ancient feast

We are near the start of the play. Romeo is talking with his friend Benvolio about being love-sick for a young maid called Rosaline. Benvolio suggests (correctly, as it turns out) that Romeo only need turn his gaze upon some other young beauty and he will be cured. Romeo maintains that he is effectively beyond remedy, worse than madly in love – at which point a Serving-man enters, bearing a letter or paper:

Benvolio:	Take thou some new infection to thy eye,	
	And the rank poison of the old will die.	50
Romeo:	Your plantain leaf is excellent for that.	
Benvolio:	For what, I pray thee?	

Romeo:	For your broken shin.
Benvolio:	Why, Romeo, art thou mad?
Romeo:	Not mad, but bound more than a madman is: 55
	Shut up in prison, kept without my food, Whipped
	and tormented, and – Good e'en, good fellow.
Serving-Man:	God gi' good e'en. I pray, sir, can you read?

(1.2.49–58)

The opening of this passage illustrates why William Hazlitt, in his *Characters of Shakespeare's Plays* (1817), suggested that 'Romeo is Hamlet in love'. Both characters seem, in Hazlitt's phrase, 'absent and self-involved' (Bate 1997, 521–522). Benvolio thinks his friend is mad. 'Your plantain leaf is excellent for that' (l.51), Romeo remarks. The obscurity of the word 'that' is compounded by the strange rejoinder that it is excellent 'For your broken shin' (l.53). Romeo seems to be saying that his sickness cannot be cured by some feeble herb: a plantain leaf might soothe a grazed shin ('broken' here refers to breaking the skin rather than the shin bone), but there is no such cure for what is afflicting Romeo. Even so, Romeo is talking in a frenzied way that invites comparison with the Shakespearean character most notorious for acting mad, namely Hamlet, Prince of Denmark. If Hamlet feels that Denmark itself is 'a prison' and imagines himself 'bounded in a nutshell' (*Hamlet*, 2.2.253–56), Romeo is 'bound more than a madman'.

Evoking the conventional Elizabethan treatment for madness, Romeo's crazed self-description ('Shut up in prison, kept without my food, / Whipped and tormented, and . . .') is only stopped by the entrance of the Serving-man. This interruption means that Romeo's outpouring here takes the rhetorical form of aposiopesis, an unfinished statement. We can never know what Romeo might have gone on to say. It is a fine example of the speed of the play, the rapidity with which Shakespeare has one thing dissolve or switch into another.

It also succinctly illustrates a more pervasive sense of things being cut off in their prime, ended before they should. This syncopation is linked to a consistent emphasis on the 'untimely', a word used five times in the play – most notably in reference to the 'untimely death' (1.4.109 and 5.3.234) of both Romeo and Juliet. This is a tragedy in which both of the eponymous lovers die before their time, not only in the sense that they are too young to die but also in the fateful irony by which each mis-times death: Romeo kills himself because he mistakenly believes that

Juliet is already dead; Juliet kills herself only after he has, on mistaken grounds, killed himself.

Romeo answers the Serving-man's question 'I pray, sir, can you read?' and the scene unfolds as follows:

Romeo:	Ay, mine own fortune in my misery.	
Serving-Man:	Perhaps you have learned it without book.	60
	But I pray, can you read anything you see?	
Romeo:	Ay, if I know the letters and the language.	
Serving-Man:	Ye say honestly, rest you merry.	
Romeo:	Stay, fellow, I can read.	
	He reads the letter.	
	'Signor Martino and his wife and daughters;	65
	County Anselme and his beauteous sisters;	
	The lady widow of Utruvio;	
	Signor Placentio and his lovely nieces;	
	Mercutio and his brother Valentine;	
	Mine uncle Capulet, his wife and daughters;	70
	My fair niece Rosaline, and Livia;	
	Signor Valentio and his cousin Tybalt;	
	Lucio and the lively Helen.'	
	A fair assembly. Whither should they come?	
Serving-Man:	Up.	75
Romeo:	Whither to supper?	
Serving-Man:	To our house.	
Romeo:	Whose house?	
Serving-Man:	My master's.	
Romeo:	Indeed, I should have asked you that before.	80
Serving-Man:	Now I'll tell you without asking. My master is	
	the great rich Capulet, and if you be not of the	
	house of Montagues, I pray come and crush a	
	cup of wine. Rest you merry. *Exit*	
Benvolio:	At this same ancient feast of Capulet's	85
	Sups the fair Rosaline, whom thou so loves,	
	With all the admirèd beauties of Verona.	
	Go thither, and with unattainted eye	
	Compare her face with some that I shall show,	
	And I will make thee think thy swan a crow.	90

(1.2.58–90)

It is sheer chance: Romeo is, as the Prologue to the play has already indicated, 'misadventured' (l.7). He will go to the 'ancient feast' and fall in love with Capulet's daughter, Juliet, only because he has inadvertently read a letter of invitation that is specifically *not addressed to him* (Romeo being, of course, 'of the house of Montagues'). We know from the passage immediately preceding this (1.2.34–4) that Juliet's father, Capulet, has just given this paper to a Serving-man, evidently forgetting (or perhaps unaware) that this Serving-man cannot read. The man has been ordered to 'trudge about, / Through fair Verona' and 'find those persons . . . / Whose names are written there' (1.2.34–6). But Romeo is so 'self-involved' (to recall Hazlitt's phrase) that he takes the Serving-man's question as an enquiry about his own inner being. 'Can you read?' he is asked. 'Ay,' he replies, 'mine own fortune in my misery.' His response encapsulates something of the strangely double and divided tone of Shakespeare's play as a whole: Romeo is being at once witty and grave, and this uncertain mixing of registers is further complicated by the way that the language shifts between the literal and the figurative.

When Romeo says 'Ay, mine own fortune in my misery', he is speaking in the conventional mode of the unrequited lover, suggesting that he can read his own fate in his unhappiness. The Serving-man may be illiterate, but he is not stupid. He recognizes that Romeo is talking figuratively and, indeed, offers a strikingly acute riposte: 'Perhaps you have learned it without book', that is to say, perhaps Romeo has learnt to read his fortune by rote or by ear, not with the physical aid of writing or a book. The Serving-man's witticism plays, once again, on the uncertainties of the literal and figurative, relying on a notion of reading distinct from the physicality of written words.

At the same time, there is a more resonant and troubling sense to be picked up in what he says, namely that being in love is a mechanical exercise, as if learnt by rote: love sickness is something that a young nobleman experiences because it is conventional to do so. A young man's feelings about the young woman with whom he is in love are not unique or uniquely tied to her. His lovesickness is a convention.

The Serving-man's remark thus reinforces what Benvolio had just, if in a more physically unpleasant metaphor, been suggesting: 'Take thou some new infection to thy eye, / And the rank poison of the old will die' (ll.49–50). It is not a matter here of supposing that the Serving-man overheard what Benvolio said, or indeed that he is making a conscious and deliberate comment on the seemingly mechanical nature of love.

To engage in a close reading of Shakespeare's play it is necessary both to acknowledge *and* to keep a critical distance from the seductive idea that the characters are actual people.

This idea warrants some further unpacking. Perhaps no one matches Shakespeare when it comes to creating characters who seem alive and singular, pulsing with an interior life, with thoughts and feelings of their own. This is why the critic Harold Bloom identifies the plays of Shakespeare with 'the invention of the human'. Our sense of self, of having an inner world of thoughts and feelings that we can articulate to ourselves, is difficult to imagine without Shakespeare, for in important respects, Bloom suggests, he has 'invented us' (Bloom 1999, xviii). He has made us what we are. Indeed, more disquietingly, Bloom contends that Shakespeare's plays 'read [us] better than [we] read them' (xx).

In irresistible ways, the characters and the language of Shakespeare's plays watch over our culture. They define what we think and how we can most critically and creatively appreciate the nature of desire, evil, love, ambition, jealousy, laughter and suffering. In Bloom's provocative summary: 'we are read by works we cannot resist. We need to exert ourselves and read Shakespeare as strenuously as we can, while knowing that his plays will read us more energetically still. They read us definitively' (xx). To read Shakespeare well is to realize that he has 'flooded [our] consciousness' (xx), endlessly prompting us to understand ourselves and others in new ways.

Bloom's argument is based on the concept of *identification*. This is why it is such a pleasure to read, to watch, to imagine a staging of, or indeed to act in, a Shakespeare play: you get to *be* that illiterate Serving-man and – even though it is just a one-liner – you get to make that fleeting but profound remark about 'learn[ing] without book'. But it is also necessary to maintain a critical guard, for the Serving-man is not real, any more than Romeo and Juliet are real. They are all in crucial respects scripted people, made out of words. The richness and complexity of Shakespeare's writing requires that we take account of this as well.

Shakespeare makes us imagine such hidden worlds. His language produces people out of thin air. But the textures and densities of his writing are even more intricate and seductive than this. For he not only conjures the hallucinatory intensity of discrete, individual characters but weaves them together in an even larger and more captivating web, which critics traditionally try to pin down with terms such as 'theme', 'imagery' and 'motif'. Such terms, however, perhaps fail to do justice to the profound weirdness of Shakespeare's writing, whereby one character's words or lines are played on and over by another's.

So, for example, the Serving-man's remark about learning love by rote eerily prefigures something Friar Lawrence says in conversation with Romeo, in Act 2 scene 3. It takes the Friar a long time to accept that Romeo has not come to him to talk about the 'fair Rosaline' by whom he was earlier so smitten, but instead to talk about another young woman, called Juliet. As if finally understanding the nature of this 'young waverer' Romeo, Friar Lawrence tells him: 'O she knew well / Thy love did read by rote, that could not spell' (2.2.87–88). In other words, Rosaline (the Friar supposes) did not return the interest Romeo showed in her because she recognized that his love was untrue (merely learnt 'by rote').

Reading Shakespeare requires careful attention to, and indeed passion for, the uncanny twists and turns of his language. The strange repetition of this image of loving 'by rote' underscores a more persistent aspect of *Romeo and Juliet*, namely the impression of love as a merely mechanical exercise. So quickly, indeed, does Romeo transfer his affections from Rosaline to Juliet that it is difficult not to feel that erotic attachment here is merely substitutive: if Juliet had not been present at the feast, some other attractive young woman would have taken his fancy. There is something faintly comical about this. It is difficult not to recall Byron's withering observation on Don Juan's adolescent infatuation: 'If *you* think 'twas philosophy that this did, / I can't help thinking puberty assisted' (*Don Juan*, Canto 1, stanza 93; Byron 1986, 401). There is a similar air of absurdity in Shakespeare's play, but also something much darker, the intimation of human desire as a sort of machine, love as mere imitation and repetition.

Afterwards

Shakespeare makes the entire 'star-crossed' tragedy of *Romeo and Juliet* turn on two chance incidents of reading that go wrong. In Act 1, scene 2 the chain of events is set in motion by Romeo happening to read a letter that is not addressed to him, and then, much later, the deadly ending of the play is brought about by the fact that another letter fails to reach its destination. Friar Lawrence's letter (apprising Romeo of the truth of Juliet's being not dead but only drugged) is 'stayed by accident' (5.3.251), before being returned to sender. The whole of the play is organized around two letters, the first of which should not have been read (but is), the second of which should have been read (but is not). To read or not to read: that is the question.

Romeo and Juliet is a dark but witty, tragic but also intermittently very funny, monumentally ironic play in which everything seems fated, destined for misfortune and death, seen in advance. Thus the Prologue to the play speaks of how we will witness 'A pair of star-crossed lovers take their life' (1.6). Romeo and Juliet are 'star-crossed' from the start. And so, in an ominous, double sense, they 'take their life': we will see how they conduct their lives, and how they commit suicide. Despite the play's relentless impression of predetermination and fatefulness, however, Shakespeare also foregrounds randomness, the aleatory or mere chance. It *can* happen that a letter gets read by someone to whom it is not addressed. It *can* happen that a letter fails to arrive at its destination. Shakespeare's *Romeo and Juliet* suggests that while there is always convention, as well as passion and desire, in a reading, there is also the unforeseeable. A good critical reading of a play will also invariably evoke something of this sense of chance, the unplanned and the unanticipated.

Every play creates a world of its own. The world of Shakespeare's *Romeo and Juliet* is radically different from the world of Sophocles's *Oedipus Rex* (c.430 BCE) or William Congreve's *The Way of the World* (1700) or Henrik Ibsen's *Hedda Gabler* (1890) or Samuel Beckett's *Endgame* (1958) or Sarah Kane's *4.48 Psychosis* (2000). But here, following on from what we have said about *Romeo and Juliet*, are seven suggestions for reading a play and preparing to write about it:

1. **Read the play.** That is the first task. But remember: notes are not just for nerds. The older a play is, the more likely you are to need an edition with explanatory notes, but in general it is always worth seeking out one with a good critical introduction and notes. You should also read as much criticism on the play as you can, without losing sight of the importance of developing your own reading. Reading a good critical essay on Beckett's *Endgame*, for example, can be invaluable in providing you not only with critical ideas to reflect upon but also with a critical model, a way of finding your own stance and voice. Arguably more than any other kinds of literature, a play gives, in Hamlet's words, 'the very age and body of the time his form and pressure' (3.2.23–24). As we have seen, *Romeo and Juliet* is set in Verona, but it is just as much about the conventions

of love and love poetry in Elizabethan England. You cannot really begin to appreciate a play such as Ibsen's *Hedda Gabler* without some historical knowledge of the position of women in late nineteenth-century society, any more than you can make sense of *Endgame* without historical awareness of the Cold War and the ubiquitous threat of atomic holocaust. A good critical edition, study guides and secondary criticism, therefore, are crucial to an understanding of a play both in detail (the meaning of a phrase) and in general (historical context).

2. **See the play.** If you cannot see it on stage or on screen, stage it in your head. Stage it in your head anyway, constantly, as you are reading. Reading a play is not just about reading the characters' words. It is also about the stage directions, props, lighting, costume, gesture, movement, music and other sound-effects.

3. **Attend to the language.** If you are reading your own copy, annotate. Bear in mind that, as with any literary text, close reading is the key. Whether it is an early modern play (such as Shakespeare's) or more contemporary work (such as Harold Pinter's or Winsome Pinnock's), be alert to the mobilization of metaphor, simile, aposiopesis, repetition, ambiguity and so on. Look out, also, for misreadings (one character, for instance, failing to understand another) and for instances of what seems unreadable, what escapes or resists reading. Above all, perhaps, try to attune your reading to a sense of irony. By this we mean not just 'dramatic irony' (where one character knows, or the audience or reader knows, something that another character doesn't know) but also the sort of self-reflexive irony that Shakespeare has in mind when he has a character suggest that 'All the world's a stage' (*As You Like It*, 2.7.139).

4. **Every play tells us about the world beyond the stage** – in the case of *Romeo and Juliet*, about the nature of love, the deadly power of names and the strangulating hold of family ('O Romeo, Romeo, wherefore art thou Romeo? / Deny thy father and refuse thy name'), the tragic potential for a message to be read by the wrong person or not to arrive at all and so on. But every play is also about playing. Every play has so-called metatheatrical or metadramatic dimensions; in other words it has things to tell us about the nature of theatre and acting. The most explicit example of this is no doubt the 'play within a play' (such as the performance of 'Pyramus and Thisbe' in *A Midsummer Night's Dream*, or 'The Mousetrap' in *Hamlet*), but a play always contains self-reflexive moments, moments in which the

audience or reader is *prompted* (to use that stagey word again) to reflect on the nature of acting and 'playing'.

5. **Every play is about the nature of desire** – starting with the spectator's or reader's identification with a character or situation and with seduction by the language of the text. Desire is never reducible to theme: desire is *in* language itself. Words and phrases ('I want you', 'I love you' and so on) can at once create and articulate, generate and intensify desire. If you enjoy a play, this inevitably has to do not just with identification (empathizing or identifying with a character), a desire or willingness to imagine yourself in his or her role, but is also fundamentally bound up with how the language of the play draws you in – with the poetic, desiring and desirable nature of the words. Any forceful reading of a play will register and often explicitly seek to analyse the dynamics of desire in the play, in the play of language, as well as in and between the bodies of characters. This is the case even if, as in Beckett's *Endgame*, two of the bodies are in dustbins or, as in Kane's *4.48 Psychosis*, it remains radically uncertain whether there are one or more bodies on stage at all.

6. **Don't just read: *act*.** Despite all the emphasis on conventions (of love, gender, class, rituals of love and death) and on the fact that, almost always, a play is scripted, the text, plot and characters known in advance, to read a play is in some sense to enact it. It is not for nothing that critics talk about an *act* of reading. To pursue a reading has a certain theatricality, a dramatic life of its own.

7. **Think about chance,** take chances. For all the scripting and convention, plays are also, like other literary works, deeply concerned with the nature of chance – with fate, coincidences, good or bad timing, the untimely and the felicitous, the surprising and unpredictable, with the randomness of life and love and death. To read a play is to immerse oneself in a play of chance, and your reading on this occasion will inevitably miss out some features and hit on others. You should aim at a reading that, in turn, has surprising and unpredictable qualities.

Further reading

Peter Brook's *The Empty Stage* (1968) is perhaps the classic modern work of criticism for thinking about the theatre. Jennifer Wallace's *The Cambridge Introduction to Tragedy* (2007) offers an excellent overview of tragedy both on and beyond the stage. In briefer mode, Adrian Poole's

Tragedy: A Very Short Introduction (2005) is also highly engaging. The inaugural critical account of 'metatheatre' is Lionel Abel's study of that title, originally published in 1963, later collected in a volume entitled *Tragedy and Metatheatre* (2004). For a good collection of essays on the topic, see Fischer and Greiner's *The Play within the Play: The Performance of Meta-Theatre and Self-Reflection* (2007). For a series of close readings of short passages in other Shakespeare plays, see Nicholas Royle, *How to Read Shakespeare* (2014). Elinor Fuchs's essay 'EF's Visit to a Small Planet' (2004) contains a rich array of questions and ideas for thinking about the world of a play. Howard Barker's *Death, the One and the Art of Theatre* (2005) is a provocative, aphoristic work about why reading a play might or should be dangerous. For a brief but informative account of Shakespeare's own reading, see Leonard Barkan's essay 'What Did Shakespeare Read?' (2001). On the idea that Shakespeare effectively shapes the nature of the modern self, see Harold Bloom's *Shakespeare* (1999). For a remarkable and richly aphoristic exploration of *Romeo and Juliet* in terms of the untimely, love, the name and irony, see Jacques Derrida's 'Aphorism Countertime' in his *Acts of Literature* (1992a). William Storm's *Irony and the Modern Theatre* (2011) provides an expansive and helpful account of its topic in work ranging from Henrik Ibsen to Tony Kushner.

6.   Reading creative non-fiction

What is creative non-fiction? Why might we care or be interested? 'Creative non-fiction', after all, sounds like a rather awkward term. It is mostly a result of publishers and editors trying – for the purposes of marketing and ease of classification – to bring together a range of distinct and often very different kinds of text. Creative non-fiction includes memoir, autobiography, life writing, blog-writing, auto-fiction, speculative non-fiction, lyric essay, creative criticism, narrative reportage, nature writing and even Unidentifiable Literary Objects. There is an obvious tension: 'creative' suggests something made up, created as if out of nothing, while 'non-fiction' implies something true, real, not fictive.

The burgeoning of creative non-fiction, in all its varieties, has been transforming literary studies over recent decades. As we try to make clear throughout this book, the study of literature is integrally bound up with uncertainty and crisis – and this, we stress, can be a good thing! The phrase 'creative non-fiction' invites us to think about truth, perhaps counter-intuitively, as bound up with some creative, inventive or imaginative activity. It draws us to reflect on the idea that the way things are, the sense of what is true, the meaning of 'non-fiction' are all things to be discovered, articulated, understood or at least approached *through writing*.

In this chapter we propose to focus on just two kinds of creative non-fiction: memoir and nature writing. Even the distinction between these two is open to question: the context for any writing is the biosphere, all memoirs are about the environment (as Samuel Beckett's Hamm says in *Endgame*, 'you're on earth, there's no cure for

DOI: 10.4324/9781003301363-7

that!' (Beckett 2006, 125)), and all nature writing has a gravitational pull towards memoir, since it necessarily entails the author's particular embeddedness in the phenomena, events, life and world that are being recorded. Some of the interconnections between memoir and nature writing will become clearer as we go on. At the same time we want to suggest that the flourishing of creative non-fiction has to do with a more general acknowledgement of larger forms of interconnectedness that shape our world (see also 'Thinking Critically' in the following section).

Memoir

A memoir is a record of events concerning a person's life: it might be the author's own life or the life of someone known personally to the writer. 'Memoir' thus has a broader sense than 'autobiography', which is a record of one's own life (the 'auto' in 'autobiography' means *self*). Moreover 'autobiography' implies, at least in principle, a narrative that covers a person's whole life, from birth up to the present time of writing, whereas a memoir tends to be fragmentary or more compartmentalized in its focus. One of the finest examples of memoir in English is Virginia Woolf's *A Sketch of the Past* (1939–40), which is (at around 80 pages in length) distinctly sketch-like, episodic, *ad hoc*.

Memoir, autobiography and the umbrella term 'life writing' all share a concern with the idea of *confession*, that is to say with both the act of confessing and the genre of confession. In this respect, one of the earliest examples of creative non-fiction is the *Confessions* of St Augustine (354–430 CE). Besides providing a stunning, page-turning account of his inner life and religious beliefs, his relationship with his mother and with the period in which he lived, Augustine acknowledges and explores the idea of *making* the truth. To confess is to 'do' or make the truth. He cites St John in the Bible: 'he who "does the truth comes to the light" (John 3: 21)' (see Augustine 1992, 179).

Confession is not wordless or ineffable: it is itself fundamentally a form of language. That is to say, it is in a very powerful sense a *speech act*. When people confess (in a court of law, in a discreet discussion with a priest or therapist, in a candid conversation with a friend at home), they are not simply saying something that is true, but they are in some sense *making the truth* specifically in the telling. Confessing goes along with other instances of so-called performative speech acts, such as naming, promising, making a bet or cursing. In producing what the philosopher

J. L. Austin (1962) calls *performative utterances*, the speaker or writer is not simply saying something, but *doing something* by saying it.

★

We might linger a moment longer on the example of *naming*. One of the classic instances of a performative is ' "I name this ship the *Queen Elizabeth*" – as uttered when smashing the bottle against the stern' (Austin 1962, 5). But we might also note how the act of naming, the promise of the name and of living up to one's name, is crucial to memoir and autobiography. Louis Chude-Sokei's memoir, *Floating in a Most Peculiar Way* (2022) is a striking example of this. He tells his life story in a series of chapters that all invoke (mostly without going into any great detail) David Bowie: 'Suffragette City', 'Absolute Beginners', 'This Is Not America', 'The Man Who Fell to Earth' and so on. Chude-Sokei draws on the name and example of someone else (David Bowie) to think about and provide a structure for understanding his own past and present.

The book is an account of Chude-Sokei's life, from genocide-shattered Biafra to the diasporic experiences of Jamaica, the United States and Nigeria. It is about a sense of identity – racial, sexual, intellectual, creative – as, in the words of Bowie's 'Space Oddity', 'floating in a most peculiar way'. But what gives his memoir its haunting integrity is, perhaps most fundamentally, the question of the name – not the name of David Bowie or indeed the author's published name of Chude-Sokei, but rather his original name as a Biafran. As Chude-Sokei observes in the final words of the narrative: 'The scars and bruises I carried were because I'd fallen to earth and had landed in a country where I could fulfill the promise of my true name' (Chude-Sokei 2022, 219). It is crucial to the poetic, enigmatic, ironic beauty of the book that the author's 'true name' is undecidably 'Onuorah' (meaning 'Voice of the People') *or* 'Onuoraegbunam' (where *egbunam* means 'Will Always Be Against Me') (see Chude-Sokei 2022, 195). The destiny promised in his name, then, is radically ambiguous: his is the voice of the people but the people will always be against him. The final words of the memoir thus leave the author truly *floating in a most peculiar way*.

The writer of a memoir or autobiography is concerned, then, not just with telling it how it is (or how it was) but with a certain creativity, with actually *creating in writing* what s/he feels, believes or knows to be true. Of course, what one person feels is true is not necessarily the same as what someone *else* feels is true. One of the great enigmas of creative non-fiction (especially the more explicitly 'personal' kind, such as memoir or life writing) has to do with the reader's difficulty in judging where or how far the author's account is true, as distinct from being just true for the author. Nonetheless, what is at stake here is the undeniable sense that, as Laura Marcus succinctly observes, 'there is a truth of "feeling" (or "fantasy") as well as of fact' (Marcus 2018, 55): such is the stuff of *non-fiction*.

Many of the points we made earlier in this book about how novels enable us to know the interior world of another or others are also relevant to how we read a work of creative non-fiction, with the important difference that the latter claims to be telling us about a real, living (or dead) person rather than about someone made up. Memoir can be compelling and seductive in turn, but for different reasons. Memoir often invites the reader to share intimate, perhaps until now private, even secret aspects of a person's past: a good memoir draws us into its own world. Up close and confiding, memoirs elicit empathy and identification. It is not by chance that the endorsements accompanying the publication of a powerful work of creative non-fiction often include descriptive phrases such as 'candid', 'immersive', 'moving', 'intimate and revealing', 'searingly honest' and 'plainspoken'.

Memoir writing often involves self-reflexive elements – an acknowledgement (or confession) that the author is struggling with language, with finding the appropriate words and being true to the subject at hand. Early on in her wonderful memoir *Giving Up the Ghost*, for example, Hilary Mantel writes:

> I hardly know how to write about myself. Any style you pick seems to unpick itself before a paragraph is done. I will just go for it, I think to myself. . . . Plain words on plain paper. Remember what Orwell says, that good prose is like a window-pane.
>
> (Mantel 2003, 4–5)

Mantel makes explicit how inextricably the self is enmeshed in the writing, how insidiously the words themselves can shape and give voice to the author, who is supposed to be in control of what she is writing.

In fact, Mantel's memoir is written in beautifully clear prose, but it's nothing like George Orwell's: it is singular, composed in a voice, style and idiom that throws its distinctive *mantle* (so to speak) over everything. And at the same time, for all its directness and clarity, *Giving Up the Ghost* remains mysterious, deceptive, enigmatic – ghostly, indeed. The title-phrase means to stop trying to do something, to acknowledge failure. It is akin to other everyday idioms such as 'chucking it in' or 'throwing in

the sponge'. But it can also mean 'dying' – which gives a darker resonance to the book from the start. And then 'giving up the ghost' can also
suggest a sort of exorcism or unburdening and thus a sense that the very
experience of writing the memoir has some cathartic or revitalising force
for the author (and perhaps also for the reader in turn).

In acknowledging that she 'hardly know[s] how to write about [her]
self', Mantel draws attention to the crucially uncertain force and effects
of words, of how much the self is entangled in – but also given the slip
by – the writing. As Virginia Woolf remarks, having just begun writing
A Sketch of the Past: 'Here I come to one of the memoir writer's difficulties – one of the reasons why, though I read so many, so many are
failures. They leave out the person to whom things happened' (Woolf
2002, 79). Lots of personal memoirs, she suggests, don't really tell us
about their subject, the person who is writing. As Woolf goes on: 'The
reason is that it is so difficult to describe any human being. So they [the
memoir-writers] say: "This is what happened"; but they do not say what
the person was like to whom it happened' (79).

★

The *creativity* of memoir, life writing or autobiography lies in the
challenge of questions such as: Who am I actually? What is a self in fact?
Is there one? Am I the same person as the person to whom the past
happened? Can this past or who am I be described in words? How am
I to reckon with the uncanny power of language in its determining, in
spite of all of my own conscious intentions and efforts, a sense of myself
that I didn't envisage or expect, or a sense of myself to which I feel foreign or perhaps remain strangely blind?

While memoir relies on story-telling, it is not constrained by issues
of plot in the same way as a novel. Whereas the plot of a novel depends
on invention, the narrative trajectories of memoir are based on the principle of selection. Perhaps even more than the novelist, the memoirist is
concerned with the tricky issue posed by E. M. Forster: 'How can I tell
what I think till I see what I say?' (Forster 1976, 99). How can I know
who I am till I've put myself into words? With memoir, it seems, what
I think (including what I think about who I am and who I have been)
is radically dependent on performative, creative effects of language over
which I have no absolute oversight or control. Creative non-fiction,
we could say, involves creative thinking in which the creative elements
would be unforeseen, unknown in advance, other to oneself.

If there is a sense that the self cannot be captured or truly evoked in language, if the memoir–writer seems unable to say 'what the person was like to whom [things] happened', the converse can also appear true: the writer seems to be talking about herself *all the time*; every word, phrase and sentence is autobiographical or 'autofictional'. Or as Paul de Man puts it, in one of his more celebrated declarations on this topic: 'any book with a readable title page is, to some extent, autobiographical' (de Man 1984, 70). Some of the most compelling memoirs are those in which the writer acknowledges this troubling *selfie-dom*, as we might call it. This is self-reflexivity not so much as textual (the text reflecting on its own peculiar status and existence) but rather as an awareness of how far our egotism extends, how much a person's sense of their environment and of other people is really just self-projection.

John Burnside's *A Lie About My Father* (2006) is a gripping, moving and at times very funny memoir about growing up with an alcoholic father. Burnside is a fine poet as well as novelist: as its title intimates, his memoir is attuned to the performative possibilities of language. A lie is a peculiar performative: it is fiction dressed up as non–fiction, a speech act aimed at avoiding or concealing the truth. What is the lie of the title? Is it a specific one-off incident? Or is it the entire memoir? Quite late on in the book we encounter these words:

> Reason, terror, unworthiness, [my father] can't even name it, it takes different guises every time, but it is always there, standing in the way, keeping him from his destiny. I'm sure my father felt these things – but these are my words, and *this* is the real lie about my father. I cannot talk about him without talking about myself, just as I can never look at myself in the mirror without seeing his face.
>
> (Burnside 2006, 231)

The memoir undergoes a small yet profound shift at this moment, as Burnside acknowledges what he calls 'the real lie about [his] father'.

Memoir is markedly personal. In a sense it is nothing but the personal. It is not, however, just a narcissistic enterprise. As Jacques Derrida has argued, 'there is not narcissism and non-narcissism, there are narcissisms that are more or less comprehensive, generous, open, extended' (Derrida 1995a, 199). Everyone is narcissistic, but what matters in the context of dignity, justice and the interconnectedness of all things, Derrida suggests, is a sense of self that is 'open to the experience of the other *as other*'

(199, emphasis added). Memoir is also a strange kettle of fish, then, insofar as it can thrive on otherness – for example, on how what might initially appear radically different transpires to be closely connected or even inseparable from oneself. Some of the most intimate and powerful memoirs are those in which the author's account is focused on what is *other than self*. In this sense, the memoir is all about *others*. It might be about a parent (as in Burnside's *A Lie About My Father*) or a grandparent (as in Lorna Sage's marvellous *Bad Blood*), for example. But it can also be about other kinds of animal, such as a whale (in the case of Rebecca Giggs's remarkable work *Fathoms: The World in the Whale*) or a bird (in the case of J. A. Baker's extraordinary *The Peregrine*).

Nature writing

Our second example of creative non-fiction is nature writing – also called environmental or eco-writing. The form overlaps with memoir since it tends to be characterized by a personal, autobiographical response and first-person narration. In nature writing, the life of the author is often intimately entwined with the nature observed. And, like memoir, it is interested in the possibility of stories and storytelling. It pushes at the boundaries of genre, and it shifts and flows between the particular and the universal.

Nature writing in English can be traced back to such luminaries as Gilbert White (1720–93) and Henry David Thoreau (1817–1862). White was a parish vicar whose *The Natural History and Antiquities of Selborne* (1789) combines careful, empirical observations on the flora and fauna of his Hampshire village with personal and impressionistic evocations. Thoreau was a philosopher, poet, transcendentalist and committed abolitionist whose voluminous writings over three decades included *Walden, or Life in the Woods* (1854) and his *Journal: 1837–1861* (posthumously published in 1906). These works intricately detail the author's experience of living in rural Concord in Massachusetts.

But there has been an extraordinary growth in the production and popularity of nature writing since the mid-twentieth century. It has given rise, indeed, to what has been called the 'new nature writing'. This burgeoning can be attributed, in large part, to the fact that our industrialized, urbanized lives are increasingly detached from our natural surroundings, as well as to our growing understanding of, and alarm about, the direct consequences of modernity: the climate crisis, ecological destruction, species extinction. We are all concerned about nature in this time of 'ecological ruination' (Macdonald 2020, 147), in these brink-days of eco-disaster. We write and read about nature because we are losing it. In the following few pages, we try to register that loss and to explore some of the ways in which nature writing responds to it.

★

A relatively early work in the 'new nature writing' tradition is Nan Shepherd's wonderfully evocative *The Living Mountain*, a book written in the 1940s about the Cairngorm mountains in Scotland but not published until 1977. Shepherd, a college lecturer who lived in the foothills of the Cairngorms, recounts her evolving relationship with the mountain range, as she wandered and climbed over it in all seasons and all weathers over many years. It is perhaps no surprise that, as Robert Macfarlane points out in his introduction to Shepherd's book, its composition – and the increasing prominence of nature writing as a genre from the mid-twentieth century onwards – coincides with the development of the philosophical movement known as phenomenology. In the work of Maurice Merleau-Ponty and Jean-Paul Sartre in particular, phenomenology emphasizes what is now often referred to as 'lived experience'.

How does Shepherd construe 'lived experience'? She notes that it would be possible to list all the birds she encounters, and that one could look up the birds in books if one wished, but that this would be to miss the point of her writing. For Shepherd, the birds 'are not in the books' but exist in 'living encounters, moments of their life that have crossed moments of mine' (Shepherd 2014, 67). Knowing or understanding the 'truth' of the mountain range involves training, discipline and learning. It is about what she calls 'quiescence': 'I too am involved', she says, in her discovery of the 'living' mountain (90).

Shepherd's impassioned observation encapsulates the importance of the *lived* encounter with nature and at the same time neatly articulates what we might identify as the paradox of nature writing. Nature writing attempts to convey an experience (of nature): in this conception, what is important is not the writing but the experience itself. The writing is simply a window, an add-on to the real thing, 'nature' itself: nature writing would ideally *efface* itself since it is merely a means of accessing the mountain, the falcon, the otter or other life-form or object. But there is a twist: it is the writing, the supplement, that brings it to our attention, allows us to access it, that makes it 'real' and brings out the 'truth' of the experience. We can only fully appreciate nature *through* writing, even while, conventionally conceived, writing is other to nature, a supplement to nature 'itself' – inessential, secondary, dispensable.

Nature writing endlessly comes up against this paradox. We might say that it governs and drives such writing. Nature writing seems compelled to be *excessive* – syntactically, rhetorically, figuratively, thematically, generically. It pushes up against its own linguistic and conceptual limits in order to gesture towards the natural world that it tries (and fails) to encapsulate or describe. And it is this rhetorical and linguistic exorbitance that marks it out from the objectivity and plainness of, say, a scientific paper on ecology, a textbook account of a geological formation, a twitcher's journal or a meteorologist's logbook – from a text or document that is primarily designed just to describe or record observable and often quantifiable facts as directly and accurately as possible.

Nevertheless, nature writing is all about the senses, and especially about seeing. Hearing can often be important, of course, as can smelling, touching, and even tasting – in addition to remembering, speculating, and imagining. It is about how sensory experience is registered cognitively, physiologically, emotionally. As Macfarlane puts it, 'Felt pressure, sensed texture and perceived space can work upon the body and so too upon the mind, altering the textures and inclinations of thought' (Macfarlane 2012, 77). But in the end, nature writing is about seeing things. And more specifically, it is about seeing *imaginatively*. As Shepherd observes 'one has to look creatively' (Shepherd 2014, 102).

One of the great nature writers of the visual is the self-confessedly myopic J.A. Baker, whose book *The Peregrine* (1967) recounts the ten years he spent following hawks and tiercels (female and male peregrines) over the Essex countryside and recording their behaviour, habitat, habits, appearance and movements. *The Peregrine* is brilliantly written, stark, obsessive and apocalyptic. 'I was possessed by [the peregrine]. It was a grail to me' (Baker 2017, 32), he remarks. And his book is highly crafted as well, compressing ten years of watching into a journal covering one unspecified and in a sense imaginary winter – from early October to early April – as Baker hunts for this supremely violent, extraordinarily skilful hunting bird. And it is all in the eye. 'The eye becomes insatiable for hawks', Baker, the 'watcher', comments (30; 140). And yet, as he also remarks, 'The hardest thing to see is what is really there' (33).

Baker's prose is both taut, economical, even minimalist, and at the same time rhetorically rich, extravagant, overwhelming. It seems to borrow from the lucid austerity of his contemporary Samuel Beckett as well as from the exuberant blood-lust of poems by Ted Hughes (Baker's prose distinctly echoes poems such as 'The Hawk in the Rain' (1957) and 'Hawk Roosting' (1960)). The writing doesn't simply describe but also strives to evoke *in language* what Baker sees. In the following paragraph, for example, animals are brought viscerally to life through the tumbling, twisting prose, as bird hunts bird:

> Screaming gulls corkscrewing high under cloud. Islands blazing with birds. A peregrine rising and falling. Godwits ricocheting across water, tumbling, towering. A peregrine following, swooping, clutching. Godwit and peregrine darting, dodging, stitching land and water with flickering shuttle. Godwit climbing, dwindling, tiny, gone: peregrine diving, perching, panting, beaten.
>
> (Baker 2017, 60–61)

Baker's prose evokes because it cannot describe: it offers a purely visual scene that a purely visual rhetoric cannot encompass. It is not a question of *seeing* this scene, in other words: it can only be written, imagined, read. Ekphrasis it is not. Nor is it simply a matter of encapsulating 'moving pictures'. It is about acknowledging – and trying to do justice to – the otherness of the birds, of movements, velocities and rhythms that are not human. As Timothy Clark remarks, 'the speed with which the world happens for a human being need not be a norm' (Clark 2011, 197).

The scene can only be 'seen' in words. And what words they are! The exorbitance of the language – the clatter of its aural effects; its repetitions; the dying fall of its final sentence; its alliteration; its repeated refusal to distinguish grammatically between gerund and participle ('tumbling, towering' and so on); its darting, syntactically incomplete phrases – takes the place of the scene (and of what is seen). And yet this verbal and grammatical excess, this exuberance of language, points to the fact that the words *cannot* finally match sense or scene – what is seen. The passage – and Baker's prose more generally – strongly suggests that writing nature is not finally possible since, as he comments later on, what is seen 'will not' – cannot – be 'meshed in words' (Baker 2017, 122).

The primary assertion of *The Peregrine* is nevertheless that it *can* somehow encompass and communicate the visible world. It is a form of visual witnessing, a way of saying – 'I saw . . . I saw . . . I saw'; 'I could see . . . I could see . . . I could see' (see, for example, Baker 2017, 63, 160: 161, 163). Even while binoculars and 'a hawk-like vigilance' reduce the disadvantage of Baker's 'myopic vision' (102), his eye repeatedly misses the target, struggles to see it. This is another major preoccupation of the book. It is about *not* seeing as much as it is about seeing: 'I could not see it' (95, 96), Baker repeatedly avers: 'I did not see it' (97); the bird 'was blurred in mist' (99). Like Shepherd, he is at pains to point out that birds on the wing, in the wild, are not like the catalogue of birds in books or their illustrations: in the wild, the observed bird is always 'sinking further back, always at the point of being lost' from view. And yet 'pictures', he insists, are effectively like 'waxworks beside the passionate mobility of the living bird' (33).

★

The environment environs not only humans: nature writing involves the questioning and active undoing of anthropocentrism. Books like Baker's push against the strangeness of the animal / human dyad, insistently moving towards while also resisting 'becoming-animal'. In a more recent book about raptors – about training rather than watching hunting birds – Helen Macdonald addresses this phenomenon directly: 'I was turning into a hawk', she says at one point'; 'Out there I forgot I was human at all' (Macdonald 2014, 84, 186). In *H is for Hawk* (2014), Macdonald tells of yearning for the distance and solitude of a bird of prey, of the desire to 'live the safe and solitary life; to look down on the world from a height and keep it there' (189). And yet it is the resistance to the anthropomorphic, sentimental impulse of imagining that we are like other animals or can ultimately imagine what it is like to be them, that drives this writing. 'My deepest relief doesn't come from imagining I can feel what the rook feels, know what the rook knows', Macdonald confesses at the end of a book of finely wrought essays on birds and other animals and life-forms: 'instead, it's slow delight in knowing I cannot'. She takes, she says, 'emotional solace from knowing that animals are *not* like me, that their lives are not about us at all' (Macdonald 2020, 258; emphasis added).

In Baker, this builds and indeed forms the narrative arc of the book, as the winter unfolds under the watcher's observant eye but also in his imagination. In the following passage, for example, he describes in starkly violent and increasingly misanthropic terms, his own identificatory metamorphosis into a peregrine. Again on this occasion, Baker is unable to locate the bird:

> Standing in the fields near the north orchard, I shut my eyes and tried to crystallize my will into the light-drenched prism of the

hawk's mind. Warm and firm-footed in long grass smelling of the sun, I sank into the skin and blood and bones of the hawk. The ground became a branch to my feet, the sun on my eyelids was heavy and warm. Like the hawk, I heard and hated the sound of man, that faceless horror of the stony places. I stifled in the same filthy sack of fear. I shared the same hunter's longing for the wild home none can know, alone with the sight and smell of the quarry, under indifferent sky. I felt the pull of the north, the mystery and fascination of the migrating gulls. I shared the same strange yearning to be gone. I sank down and slept into the feather-light sleep of the hawk. Then I woke him with my waking.

(Baker 2017, 148)

Baker's astonishing prose presses against the limits of sense, with phrases such as 'crystallize my will', 'long grass smelling of sun', 'a branch to my feet', 'I stifled in', 'slept into the feather-light sleep' – phrases that chime, in their subtle distortions, with poetry as much as with the conventions of prose. It's as if, in imaginatively becoming animal, one is moving decisively away from conventional coherent sense into the outer reaches of poetic language. As Timothy Clark wonders, 'What is the "literal" language for describing the behaviour of an animal?' (44).

There is a distinctive poetic rhythm and cadence in Baker's phrasing, along with the almost-anagrammatic alliteration of 'heard' / 'hated' and the affective intensity of 'I stifled in the same filthy sack of fear'. And the passage takes on weighty existential questions when it refers, for example, to the 'indifferent sky'. But above all it insistently moves through a series of verb-clauses that, while they identify the speaker with the bird and thereby distance him from a feared and hated humanity, also mark a tragically unbridgeable distance from the animal as such – 'I sank into . . .', 'I stifled', 'I shared', 'I felt', 'I shared', 'I sank down' . . . and then 'I woke him with my waking'.

Part of this has to do with the fundamental impossibility of articulating the alterity of the bird, of bird life, to register the sense that, as the writer Philip Hoare puts it, birds exist 'apart from us: unmammalian, and therefore uncanny' (Hoare 2017, 35). And it is partly the very fact of human language itself that sets us apart from other animals. We can talk about animals, as if knowingly, but in doing so we mark our difference from them. As Macdonald remarks, it is a 'curious blend of familiarity and otherness that we see in wild creatures' (Macdonald 2020, 199).

★

The strangeness of the non-human world, then, is that it is finally beyond language. To think it, this world, one needs what Peter Boxall calls 'an expanded mechanism of likeness', which is also 'a new, nonhuman adhesion between things in the universe' (Boxall 2020, 344). This is perhaps why writers like Baker resort so often to extraordinary metaphors and similes. Just as the Romantic poet Percy Bysshe Shelley can only rely on a series of similes to describe the skylark and its song in 'To a Skylark' (1820) ('Like a cloud of fire . . . Like an unbodied joy . . . Like a start of Heaven . . . Like a Poet . . . Like a high-born maiden . . . Like a glow-worm . . . Like a rose embower'd'), Baker incessantly exploits the power of language to say what something is *like* because it lacks the capacity to say what or how it *is*: Sparrowhawks are 'always near me in the dusk, like something I meant to say but could never quite remember' (Baker 2017, 29); the peregrine's eyes 'shine wet in the sunlight, like circles of raw liver' (49); a bird sinks 'slowly down . . . lowering like a threaded spider from the web his wings had spun' (52); another floats 'lightly . . . like a drifting sycamore seed' (52) and so on.

In the end, nature is that which, as Timothy Clark puts it, is 'in no need of further justification' (Clark 2011, 69). Nature writing is impelled by ecological crisis. These are 'terrible times for the environment', Helen Macdonald comments, and part of the power of nature writing is that it can 'communicate what these losses mean' since it can 'teach us the qualitative texture of the world' (Macdonald 2020, ix). Writing in the 1960s, Baker too was aware of and angry about environmental destruction (see Baker 2017, 32, 216). But in the imaginative, creative power of his writing, he also revels in nature for itself. Ultimately, it is indeed the pointlessness of nature writing and the pointless power and beauty of nature that most compellingly makes the case for our attention to, and care for, the world in which we live and must die.

We will conclude this section with a passage from Baker's notebooks about the song of woodlarks late at night in the 'wet woods'. What he says may not be ornithologically orthodox (there are perfectly good territorial and reproductive reasons for birds to sing), but the passage is magisterial, nevertheless, in its response to what it sees as the sheer sublime art-like pointlessness, the 'non-sense', of birdsong:

> And a feeling of great exhilaration possessed me, like a sudden lungful of purer air. The great pointlessness of it, the non-sense of nature, was beautiful, and no-one else would know it again, exactly as we knew that moment. Only a bird would circle high in the darkness,

endlessly singing for pure untainted, instinctive joy, and only a bird-watcher would stand and gorp at something he could never hope to see, sharing that joy.

(Baker 2010, 274)

Summary

Creative non-fiction can be characterized, and distinguished from non-fiction in general, by:

- the prominence of an autobiographical authorial 'I';
- the development and self-awareness of a specific narrative 'voice';
- an attentiveness to narrative form, especially to storytelling that is not end-directed or teleological;
- surprising kinds and a surprising degree of imagination, of invention, as well as of observation;
- a marked interest in thematic complexity and connectiveness;
- craft: creative non-fiction shapes and crafts a narrative rather than just recording or recounting events;
- an exploration of the possibilities of genre and a tendency to value 'generic disobedience' (Macfarlane 2014, xi);
- verbal and rhetorical extravagance;
- an engagement with philosophical questions, especially as an interanimation of the particular and the universal;
- a self-conscious registering of the positionality and intrusiveness of the writer.

Further reading

Although directed more towards the practitioner than the critic, Margot Singer and Nicole Walker's collection of essays on the craft of creative non-fiction, *Bending Genre: Essays on Creative Nonfiction* (2023), is a good place to start. Two excellent introductory books on autobiography as a literary genre are Linda Anderson's *Autobiography* (2011) and Laura Marcus's *Autobiography: A Very Short Introduction* (2018). In a more philosophical vein, Adriana Cavarero's *Relating Narratives: Storytelling and Selfhood* (2000) is brilliant, and thought-provoking, on the idea that selves are formed around the stories that people tell themselves about themselves, but that one *can't* finally tell one's own story (not least because you can't know your own beginning – or your end). Robert Macfarlane's introduction to Nan Shepherd's *The Living Mountain* includes a brief explanation of the influence of phenomenology (and especially Maurice Merleau-Ponty) on Shepherd's book and on nature writing more generally (see xxvii–xxix in Macfarlane 2014). You will find the classic statement of 'becoming-animal' in Gilles Deleuze and Félix Guattari, *A Thousand Plateaus*, ch.10 (2013) (the chapter is also available in Kalof and Fitzgerald, eds. (2007)). Richard Mabey's *The Oxford Book of Nature Writing* (1995) offers a wide range of excerpts from 'classic' writing in the genre from the Ancient Greeks to the late twentieth century, while Timothy Morton's challenging but brilliant *Ecology without Nature* (2007) argues against the value of using the word 'nature' at all.

Part II
Thinking

7. Thinking about literature

Literature is not what you think.
Everything in this book, we hope, points in that direction.
In this chapter we would like to offer some thoughts about literature.

1. Thinking about literature involves thinking about thinking

Thinking about literature – what we are doing in writing this book, what you are doing in reading it, and what one does in reading, talking about and writing on poems, plays, novels – also involves thinking about how literary texts think about thinking, the kinds of thinking they do, and the kinds of thinking that one does in reading and thinking about them.

2. Thinking about literature is thinking about everything in the world

There are no limits to what literature might be 'about'; literature can be about anything in the world. And it can be about what is not in the world, what is outside it, and about other worlds or no worlds. We're not just talking about fantasy fiction or sci-fi here, but more generally about the so-called 'world' of imagination or invention, for example.

3. Thinking about literature involves thinking about social justice

The very stuff of literature, its subject-matter, is our world, in all its incoherence, injustice, prejudice, discrimination and inequality. Social justice – and

DOI: 10.4324/9781003301363-9

social *injustice* – is just what literature is about. We are confronted, in reading books, with thoughts of how profoundly unjust our world is – and of how we might imagine it (and think about making it) a better place.

4. Thinking about literature allows you to think another person's thoughts

Your mind is no longer only your own in reading a literary text. Thinking about literature allows you to be taken over by another mind, by alien thoughts. You have the exhilarating, extravagant, liberating, enthralling but also disquieting possibility of being other to yourself, imagining yourself in previously unimagined places and ways.

5. Thinking about literature can also entail not thinking

The speaker in one of the most famous lyric poems in English, John Keats's 'Ode on a Grecian Urn' (1820), looks longingly, even enviously, at an ancient Greek urn. The urn is so quietly, implacably beautiful, and so mysterious, he thinks. And as he sighs, or complains, or enthuses, it 'tease[s] us out of thought' (1.44). It overwhelms him. We might understand Keats's speaker to be representing not only a person looking at an urn but also a person reading an artwork or poem. In which case, here is a thought: when we read a poem, or when we read a certain kind of poem, we are not so much thinking as *not* thinking, being teased *out* of thought, as well as into it. The strange, heady sense of not thinking, of thought stopped.

6. Thinking about literature teases us into thought

The slightly wider context of Keats's comment about being teased out of thought might help to clarify it. The speaker in the poem is not only contemplating but actually addressing the urn:

> Thou, silent form, dost tease us out of thought
> As doth eternity . . .

What does this mean? Why is the speaker saying this? Perhaps we can try to tease out the thought. The speaker says that the urn teases him 'out of thought' because it is 'like' eternity. 'Dost' and 'doth' were archaic, and therefore poetic, forms of the word 'does', even in Keats's time, just as 'thou' is a poeticism for 'you'. These archaisms underscore a sense of ancientness, of extension across time. We might surmise that the urn is like eternity because it has lasted a very long time: it therefore seems 'eternal' by comparison with the relatively brief life-span of a human being. But how does it 'tease' us? One way to read the verb 'tease' is as a kind of mockery: we feel as if an ancient work of art 'mocks' us because it reminds us of our mortality, of the really very limited extent of our time on this earth – the several-thousand-year life-span of the urn makes a mockery of our three-score-years-and-ten.

But we might say that the urn 'teases' the speaker in another way. The *OED* notes that the original sense of 'tease' is 'To separate or pull asunder the fibres of; to comb or card (wool, flax, etc.) in preparation for spinning; to open out by pulling asunder; to shred' (*OED* 'tease', v1: 1.a.). Like infinity, the concept of eternity messes with your head, pulls it asunder. The novelist David Foster Wallace published a primer on the mathematics of infinity in which he stressed just this: thinking, really thinking, about infinity, you can very quickly feel 'a strain at the very root of yourself, the first popped threads of a mind starting to give at the seams' (Wallace 2005, 24). So perhaps the speaker in Keats's poem is teased 'out of thought' because of how the urn makes him think about eternity or the infinite. He is teased out of thought by being teased into it. And perhaps novels and poems and plays are 'teasing' in this way too – in the way the urn is teasing to the speaker in Keats's poem.

7. Thinking about literature is thinking about nothing

Keats offers some intriguing and provocative thoughts about thinking in another short poem, a fourteen-line sonnet known by its first line, 'When I have fears that I may cease to be' (written in 1818). The titular first line of Keats's sonnet announces the subject of the poem – a person thinking about his own imminent death (as it happens, Keats died only three years after writing these words, at the age of twenty-five). When I think about dying, the speaker seems to be saying, and when I think of dying before I have managed to write all the poems in my 'teeming brain', or when I think that my death will mean that I will never see my lover again, then I feel as though I am standing alone on the metaphorical 'shores' of the world, thinking, just thinking – thinking in what seems to be an abstract, empty way. And when I think in this way, the speaker says, questions of fame and love appear to 'sink' into nothingness, into oblivion.

Keats puts it better than we do, though (he is the famous poet, after all):

> When I have fears that I may cease to be
> Before my pen has gleaned my teeming brain,
> Before high-pilèd books, in charactery,
> Hold like rich garners the full ripened grain;
> When I behold, upon the night's starred face,   5
> Huge cloudy symbols of a high romance,
> And think that I may never live to trace
> Their shadows with the magic hand of chance;
> And when I feel, fair creature of an hour,
> That I shall never look upon thee more,   10
> Never have relish in the faery power
> Of unreflecting love – then on the shore
> Of the wide world I stand alone, and think
> Till love and fame to nothingness do sink.
>
> (Keats 1988, 221)

Keats uses the work 'think' twice in this sonnet, the first time rather unremarkably in line 7 but the second time in a powerful instance of enjambment in the penultimate line. With this final 'think' in line 13, everything is suspended, up in the air. Despite the fact that the line runs on to the next (there is no punctuation after 'think'), we are invited to think about 'think' as an end in itself. In this sense the speaker seems not actually to be thinking *about* anything at all. The thought here, the thinking, is empty. The thinking is empty, but it puts the world into a different perspective, makes everything – even love and fame – nothing. And that's saying something, since these are Keats's greatest loves, really: he loves love and, like any star-struck youth, he would love to have been famous. Which he wasn't – not until after his death, that is.

8. Thinking about literature is virtual thinking

Literature is virtual, like online gaming or a movie. In some sense, it is even more 'virtual' than these because there are no sights or sounds involved. Everything that takes place in the book takes place inside your head. There is nothing to see, or hear. Even the particular configuration of the words on the page, how the words look, is, for most texts most of the time, quite incidental, quite separate from their existence as poems or novels. For the most part, a poem or novel can be printed in Times New Roman, or **Bernard MT Condensed**, or *Vladimir Script*, and can be recited or remembered 'by heart', but it will make no *essential* difference to the poem as a poem or novel as a novel. In this sense, poems or novels (unlike paintings, say, or ancient Greek urns, which seem to lose something intrinsic to their status as works of art when copied) are infinitely reproducible.

There are, of course, important exceptions to that rule, and those exceptions might give us pause with regard to any literary text, in fact. We are thinking in particular of how the so-called 'concrete' or 'visual' works of such poets as George Herbert (1593–1633) or Edwin Morgan (1920–2010) powerfully foreground the materiality of writing itself. Below and on the next page is an example of a 'visual' poem by Herbert, 'Easter-Wings', where the shape of the poem on the page mirrors its title and topic, wings (wings figuring metonymically as flight). In this poem, the poet talks about 'imping' (grafting or implanting) his wings on those of Christ, and the shape of the stanzas on the page mimic a bird's wings (a lark's, for example) as if the page, like the poet himself, might take flight with the resurrected Christ at Easter:

LORD, who createdst man in wealth and store,
        Though foolishly he lost the same,
            Decaying more and more,
                Till he became
                Most poore:
                With thee
            O let me rise
        As larks, harmoniously,
    And sing this day thy victories:
Then shall the fall further the flight in me.

My tender age in sorrow did beginne:
    And still with sicknesses and shame
        Thou didst so punish sinne,
            That I became
            Most thinne.
            With thee
        Let me combine,
    And feel this day thy victorie,
For, if I imp my wing on thine,
Affliction shall advance the flight in me.

(Herbert 2007, 147)

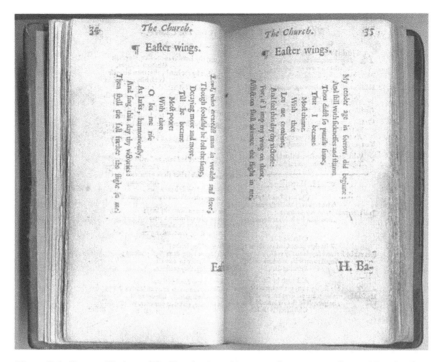

Figure 7.1 George Herbert, *The Temple: Sacred Poems and Private Ejaculations* (Cambridge, 1633), pp. 34–35.

In its first publication in *The Temple* (1633), the lines were printed at 90 degrees to bring out the wing-shaped materiality of the printed page more powerfully. The effect is to draw the reader's attention to the sheer shape of the words on the page and indeed to obstruct the act of reading (in effect you have to turn the book to read the words; see Figure 7.1).

9. Thinking about literature is like thinking about silent film

The 2011 Michel Hazanavicius film *The Artist* reminded those who had forgotten or who had never seen them, that watching early twentieth-century silent films does not so much involve a *loss* of something (sound-effects, speech) as the gain of a different kind of experience. Most people, on watching the early twenty-first-century (mostly) silent film

The Artist, seem quite quickly to get over their initial disappointment on finding that the words that the actors speak to each other cannot be heard because they soon become engrossed, involved in the visual spectacle of the film. As they watch the film, audiences feel not so much that speech and sound are withheld but that they are involved in a wholly different way of experiencing a narrative. The plot of *The Artist* is all about this feature of silent movies, in fact, based as it is on the historical resistance to the 'talkies' – films with sounds – in the late 1920s and early 1930s (strange as it may seem today, the 'talkies' were seen by many as a degraded, hybrid, populist form, technologically flash-in-the-pan and aesthetically preposterous). Something similar is at work when we read literary texts. Once you have put away the TV, the computer game, the hyperlinked hand-held reading device, the internet, it is possible to be absorbed by the alternative pleasures of reading – pleasures that are in fact limitless, that are constrained only by the limits of your imagination. The events described in books exist in one's head and in ways that are infinitely richer than those offered by other, apparently more immediate forms of representation.

10. Thinking about literature should be exacting

Talking and writing about literature is not just a question of expressing yourself or your ideas: it calls for structure, control and critical precision. There are certain broadly accepted if never entirely uncontested protocols or 'rules' of reading and criticism. Here are a few of the most important and least controversial ones:

- speakers in lyric poems or first-person novels should never be taken naively, unthinkingly, for authors themselves;
- the way that something is expressed in a poem or novel is a fundamental part of what it means;
- your reading of a text is never simply, unproblematically yours, yours alone (it should always be justifiable, explainable, based on evidence from the text that can be shared with others);
- literary texts cannot be reduced to unified or univocal, identifiable, extractable meanings;
- literary texts relate to each other as well as to the world of which they are a part;
- literary texts are historical documents, even while they can be read in different ways at different times in different contexts;

- literary texts prompt us to think about philosophical questions, such as: What is love? What is the value of revenge? How far and in what ways does language determine our lives? What's in a name?

11. Thinking about literature involves thinking about feeling

. . . or thinking with feeling. The two are intimately bound up with each other, of course: you can't think about your mother or your cat or your future, without feeling *something*, and probably quite a lot of things. And since literature tends vividly to bring to life pretty much everything under the sun (including some really quite difficult stuff like sex and death, love and hatred, jealousy and resentment, tragedy, war and disaster), it's not surprising that the thoughts it brings up are often powerfully emotive.

12. Thinking about literature is embodied

If we think with feeling, we also think with our bodies, in our bodies. After all, the organic matter that we think with is itself in and part of our body, and being embodied is not only the consistent subject-matter of literary texts but an intimate dimension of our response to the literary work. We relate to literature in the first place through our bodies.

13. Thinking about literature is not thinking about any old thing

There is no 'thing' that is literature. This is not to say that there are no poems, plays, stories or novels (why would you say that?) but that there is no stable, coherent, identifiable single object that one can point to or name when one talks about 'literature'. This thing called literature is very strange – ghostly, elusive, at once more and less than a thing.

14. Thinking about literature prompts you to think ultimate thoughts

Thinking can be a problem in the sense that – outside hunger, violence, poverty, environmental destruction – human trouble begins in thoughts.

'There is nothing either good or bad but thinking makes it so', as the self-torturingly philosophical, over-thinking Hamlet comments to Rosencrantz and Guildenstern (*Hamlet* 2.2.251–252).

But then not thinking or not being able to think is also a problem. Philip Larkin dwells on the prospect of the end of thinking in one of his late poems, 'Aubade' (1977), a poem about the fear of never thinking again because one is dead (Larkin 2012, 115–116). Traditionally, an 'aubade' is a poem about two lovers parting in the morning. More generally, it names a poem set in the morning, at day-break, and in particular one that dwells on a parting. The speaker in Larkin's poem talks about waking at four in the morning and seeing 'what's really always there': 'Unresting death, a whole day nearer now' (ll.4–5). Larkin's 'Aubade' is a morning poem about the inevitability that one will eventually part from life itself. For Larkin, or for the speaker in this poem at least, this thought of the inevitability of death is almost unbearable. The anticipation of death makes 'all thought impossible' (l.6) except the blank, content-less, unanswerable thought of death itself: 'The mind blanks at the glare', he says, there is 'nothing more terrible, nothing more true' (ll.11, 20). Neither religion (with its 'pretence' that 'we never die' (l.24)) nor reason (with the argument that you cannot logically fear what you will not feel) can offer him consolation. Indeed it is precisely the *thought* of being nothing, of not experiencing anything, that terrifies the speaker. What he fears is precisely that there will be:

> . . . no sight, no sound,
> No touch or taste or smell, nothing to think with,
> Nothing to love or link with,
> The anaesthetic from which none come round.
>
> (ll.27–30)

In a terrible irony, then, it is thinking that brings the speaker to this point at four in the morning, but it is the prospect of not thinking that he fears. Where else would you be brought to think about this thinking, this kind of thinking, if not in a literary text? Where else would the rhyme of 'think with' and 'link with' work so forcefully and poignantly to connect thinking with the way that we link, or fail to link, with others? And where else, indeed, can you think so richly and so movingly about death and about the fear of dying? What other space would there be for such thoughts? Not a doctor's surgery, certainly – too clinical, medical. Not a morgue – too impersonal, refrigerated. Not a crematorium – too heart-rending, mournful, grief-ridden. Not a church or mosque or synagogue – too spiritual, dogmatic, theological. Not a philosophy seminar – too cerebral, theoretical, abstract. Not an analyst's couch – too personal, individual, expensive. Not even on TV or in a film, we would suggest, since these are too visual, momentary, immediate.

15. Thinking about literature is not an order

We are not saying: *think* about literature! We are not trying to emulate Samuel Beckett's Pozzo.

'Think, pig!', cries Pozzo to a slave-like and truly unlucky character called Lucky in Beckett's *Waiting for Godot* (1953). Pozzo orders him about and holds him by a leash around the neck, like a dog or a performing bear. He boasts to Vladimir and Estragon that Lucky can perform a dance and that he can also perform 'thinking aloud': 'Think!', Pozzo orders, and then again, 'Think!' And out comes a five-minute philosophico-religious disquisition, a jumble of words and a word-like jumble of sounds, from the mouth of Lucky (Beckett 2006, 41–43).

But whether Lucky can be said to be thinking is unclear. Can one think to order? Would that not simply be an *enactment* of thinking? If you merely *perform* thinking, are you in fact thinking, really thinking, at all? One of the thoughts that the scene seems to prompt is that thinking cannot be forced, that you cannot order someone to think. Given the right implements or tools, or drugs, or electrodes, or given enough social and political power, or money, or enough film directors and actors, you can no doubt force someone to believe and say certain things or to believe or speak in certain ways. Totalitarian states, with their usually rather well-paid secret police, have some success at this, as do religious organizations, advertising agencies, and some teachers and parents. Global capitalism, that vague, but hauntingly pervasive web-like phenomenon, is monumentally, world-historically effective at making people think certain thoughts – that you should buy things 'because you're worth it', for example, or that 'freedom' means the freedom to pursue personal happiness unencumbered by consideration for the starving, for the oppressed or indeed for the planet.

But there is a question of whether the person who has been forced or persuaded to 'think' in certain ways is actually *thinking* at all – as opposed simply to repeating certain patterns of thought, or certain phrases and ideas. People often talk scathingly about the 'thought police' or about 'brainwashing' in this context. George Orwell famously dramatized just this question of thinking in his dystopian novel *Nineteen Eighty-Four* (1949), which depicts a totalitarian society dominated by the 'Thought Police', whose job it is to punish 'thoughtcrime' committed by 'thought-criminals'. To make people think, to make them really think, however, would be a different matter entirely. It would constitute something of a paradox or double bind – like the order 'Think for yourself!', which is impossible to obey, if you think about it. If you obey the order to think for yourself, then you are not thinking for yourself and therefore not obeying the order. (Did you just think that? Or did we? Or was it the British anthropologist Gregory Bateson, who coined the term 'double bind' in the 1950s (see Bateson 1973, 178–179)?)

In a brief war-time essay called 'The Frontiers of Art and Propaganda' (1941), Orwell argued that while literature is political, it should not simply constitute a branch of the propaganda machine, that it should not, and properly speaking does not, say: think this! Or even 'Think, pig!', or 'Think!' Rather, literature says something like: here is a thing (a person, an event, an object, a story, a poem, a scene, an image, an idea, an arrangement of words, a metaphor); what do you think about it?

16. Reading literature, and thinking about it, is one of life's great pleasures

So let's start reading – and thinking . . .

Further reading

Thinking is itself a lively topic in recent literary criticism. In relation to thinking about 'the body', 'pleasure' and 'feelings', in particular, you might want to look at the chapters on these topics in Bennett and Royle (2023). In *Thinking Without Thinking in the Victorian Novel* (2012), Vanessa Lyndal Ryan has produced a fascinating examination of the question of Victorian writers' engagements with and representations of the emerging physiology and neurology of the unconscious, while Gregory Tate's *The Poet's Mind: The Psychology of Victorian Poetry, 1830–1870* (2012) focuses on the emerging field of psychology as it is reflected in poetry of the period. For some rigorous and challenging thinking about thinking in literature, see Anthony Uhlmann's *Thinking in Literature: Joyce, Woolf, Nabokov* (2011), and Sharon Cameron's *Thinking in Henry James* (2009). Although we do not focus on it specifically in this chapter, cognitive science has recently had a significant impact on literary studies (sometimes referred to as the 'cognitive turn'). A good place to start is Lisa Zunshine's collection of essays on various aspects of the topic by some of the leading practitioners, *Introduction to Cognitive Cultural Studies* (2010). More specifically focused on storytelling and the brain, neuroscience and AI, see also Angus Fletcher's clear and engaging *Storythinking: The New Science of Narrative Intelligence* (2023). On the other hand, if you take Avital Ronell's point that literary language has to do with the '*failure* of cognition', then her fascinating and inventive, if also demanding, book *Stupidity* (2002) will be of interest. See, too, Stathis Gourgouris's *Does Literature Think? Literature as Theory for an Antimythical Era* (2003), with its brilliant recognition that 'the way that literature thinks casts into all sorts of turbulence the status of the act of thinking'.

8.   Thinking critically

What does it mean to think critically? How is such thinking at the heart of literary studies? What do you do with what other people think, in other words with the critical or theoretical material you read, also known as 'secondary sources'? These are some of the questions we will explore in the following pages.

Crisis thinking

The words 'criticism' and 'crisis' both come from the ancient Greek verb *krinein*, to judge, to discern, to cut. The word 'critical' has to do with making judgements and decisions: all literary criticism worthy of the name is in crisis and always has been. No wonder students sometimes talk about having an essay crisis. But while the critical may be about cutting off, discerning and delivering judgements, 'thinking' appears, on the contrary, to have no end. Are there limits? When or how can you stop thinking?

The idea that thinking is interminable can be a source of immense pleasure and reassurance: 'Whatever happens, I can always go on thinking – no one can take *that* away from me', you may think to yourself. And the fact that you can think this to yourself and that no one else can know may be a great solace.

But thinking can also be disturbing, even terrifying. This is what T.S. Eliot dramatizes at one moment in *The Waste Land*, when he has a voice (usually taken to be female) say: 'What are you thinking of? What thinking? What? / I never know what you are thinking. Think' (Eliot 1963, 57). It is the lover's perennial question – the subject of a

DOI: 10.4324/9781003301363-10

more-or-less unremitting curiosity – to know what their partner is thinking (about you).

Then there is the double bind that we encountered at the end of the last chapter: *think*. No one likes being told what to think, even if we are quite accustomed to encountering such messages in everyday life ('Think of the consequences', 'Think for yourself' or, in more negative mode, 'Don't even think about it'). At the same time, Eliot's lines carry out a sort of thinning out and wearing down ('What are you thinking of? What thinking? What?') that makes the concluding imperative, 'Think', resound with a certain madness.

When you start thinking about thinking, then, it can become dizzying. You may want to stop. But the thought of thinking coming to a complete stop is itself disturbing. Elizabeth Bowen evokes such a stopping of thought in the marvellous opening sentences of her first novel, *The Hotel* (1927):

> Miss Fitzgerald hurried out of the Hotel into the road. Here she stood still, looking purposelessly up and down in the blinding sunshine and picking at the fingers of her gloves. She was frightened by an interior quietness and by the thought that she had for once in her life stopped thinking and might never begin again.
>
> (Bowen 1943, 5)

Happily, you are not Miss Fitzgerald: she is a character in a work of fiction. And what particularly marks out these sentences as fiction, of course, is the fact that what we are being given here is 'the thought' of a fictional being. One of the distinguishing features of novels is that they offer us what Dorrit Cohn calls 'transparent minds' (Cohn 1978), the thoughts or 'interior quietness' of other people. And to think critically about a novel is, as we have argued in 'Reading a novel', to acknowledge the ways in which thinking in a novel, characters thinking, is a fabrication, a pretence, a fiction.

Patience and impatience

So when it comes to thinking and writing critically, it is a matter of trying to keep thinking open, of seeing how in truth you cannot be Miss Fitzgerald even if (for some bizarre reason) you wanted to be: *you cannot stop thinking*. Even the fear of having 'stopped thinking' is still, as Bowen emphasizes, a thought. Thinking critically entails being attentive to the ways in which thinking cannot end: any good critical essay (or indeed good seminar discussion) makes this clear. It makes you think, leaves you thinking. At the same time, when you are reading or taking notes or actually in the process of writing an essay, you have to deal with the constraints and frameworks you are given, and therefore impose cuts, make decisions, pass judgement.

In order to sum up these tensions we might consider a remark by Franz Kafka:

> All human errors are impatience, a premature breaking-off of methodical procedure, an apparent fencing-in of what is apparently at issue.
>
> (Kafka 1994, 3)

In the context of literary studies, this sentence is perhaps especially valuable when you need to organize your thoughts and start writing. Be patient. Be methodical. Beware the deceptiveness of appearances. Kafka's repetition here ('apparent', 'apparently') alerts us to the necessarily tentative or provisional nature of all thinking, critical or otherwise.

Kafka's sentence is an example of an aphorism, that is to say, a resonant statement that seems to convey the truth in an arresting and memorable way. An aphorism is literally a fencing-in, a cutting off of the horizon (from the ancient Greek *apo*, 'from', and *horos*, 'limit' or 'horizon'). As Gabriel Josipovici puts it, aphorisms give us 'in lapidary form what everyone knows but few have been clear-sighted and skilful enough to express' (in Kafka 1994, vi). Or, more aphoristically, they give us 'What oft was thought, but ne'er so well expressed', to recall Alexander Pope's celebrated definition of wit from 1711 ('An Essay on Criticism', l.298 (Pope 2006, 27)).

Aphorism, then, is a distilled form of critical thinking. Many major authors are also brilliant aphorists. We might think of Sappho, Blaise Pascal, Alexander Pope, William Blake, Emily Dickinson, Friedrich Nietzsche, Oscar Wilde, Kahlil Gibran, Dorothy Parker, Wallace Stevens, Ludwig Wittgenstein, Jacques Derrida or Sarah Manguso.

While 'thinking critically' is not the same as 'thinking aphoristically', it is not a bad idea to try, at some point in your reading or writing about a text or author, to come up with an aphorism of your own, a way of saying what is, for you, most striking, important, thought-provoking, strange or amusing about the text or author you are working on. If you are able to come up with such a statement, this can prove invaluable for drawing your ideas together and enabling you to see how your reading or essay writing might be structured and organized. The aphorism you arrive at may be especially useful in getting you started on an essay or in providing you with a conclusion, or both. Assembling your critical thinking in the form of an aphorism is also a short sharp lesson in self-expression: it forces you to come to some sort of judgement, to put the point in a way that matters to you.

But no one gets to be as witty as Pope, as smart as Wittgenstein, as funny as Wilde, as pithy as Parker or as haunting as Kafka overnight. Thinking critically is something that comes, first and foremost, from engaging with the critical thinking of others. In his *Tractatus Logico-Philosophicus* (1921), Wittgenstein remarks: 'Everything that can be thought at all can be thought clearly. Everything that can be put into words can be put clearly' (Wittgenstein 1961, 4.116). Reading philosophical, theoretical or indeed critical texts is crucial to developing an ability to think critically, to clarifying what and how you think.

In a panicked sense that there is nothing new to say, one might overlook secondary sources (critical essays, works of philosophy or theory). But this would be a mistake. Some of the best critical thinking comes from picking up and bouncing off what other critics or writers, philosophers or theorists have written. Engaging with the critical thinking of others is the quickest way of realizing that you are not alone and of clearing a space for self-discovery, of finding out what you think.

In this context, we might consider an aphorism from Oscar Wilde's heart-rending account of homosexual love, his trial and imprisonment, in *De Profundis* (written in Reading Gaol in 1897): 'Most people are other people. Their thoughts are someone else's opinions, their life a mimicry, their passions a quotation' (Wilde 2013, 118). The first sentence here is deceptively light. It might initially seem obvious, even a kind of tautology: people are not me, they are other people. But Wilde's second sentence comes to modify this: more playfully but also perhaps more profoundly, he is suggesting that most people are not themselves, they are other *to themselves*, other people. There is something archetypally Wildean in this paradox ('What the paradox was to me in the sphere of thought', the queer Wilde remarks in the same text, 'perversity became to me in the sphere of passion' (101)). For Wilde, most people do not have their own thoughts, they merely imitate others. Even their most intense experiences or 'passions' are 'a quotation'.

Wilde's formulation may highlight the feeling that, as the Bible says, 'There is no new thing under the sun' (Ecclesiastes, 1.9), but it gives an added twist in accentuating the extent to which this is bound up with language itself ('opinions' and 'quotation'). There is something witty and ironic, too, about Wilde's phrasing: is he here expressing what he himself really thinks? Or is this aphorism not also an opinion, the eminently quotable expression of a passion, as if it were indeed 'someone else's'? (It echoes Arthur Rimbaud's renowned aphorism, *Je est un autre* – 'I is another' (Rimbaud 1966, 305).) Are you different from 'most people' or not? We might rephrase this paradox: if you want to think critically, you need to think for yourself, and the best way of doing this is by reading other people.

If literature is, at least in principle, the space in which it is possible to say anything in any way, good critical thinking and critical writing seeks to reckon with this. Critical writing, like the writing of drama, poetry or creative non-fiction, should be an adventure of thought. At least when you write the first draft of an essay, you should be willing to make horrible mistakes, to lurch off in unexpected directions that may in the end prove quite fruitless.

As the philosopher Martin Heidegger rather grandly posits: 'He who thinks greatly must err greatly' (Heidegger 1975, 9). Or as Alexander Pope epigrammatically puts it in his 'An Essay on Criticism' (a poem largely about errors and erring): 'To err is human, to forgive, divine' (1.525) (Pope 2006, 33). Take it from us: there is comfort in these thoughts. Thinking critically emerges at least in part from taking paths you perhaps did not even realize existed before you started writing. Again we might recall a critical observation made by Elizabeth Bowen: 'To write is to be captured – captured by some experience to which one may have hardly given a thought' (Bowen 1986, 125). So along with the focus on what other people say and on how you find what they say valuable, evocative, problematic, only partially helpful, rich, eloquent, memorable, original, contentious, hyperbolic, insufficient, illuminating and so on, and along with the critical ideas and arguments that you have noted with regard to the primary text or texts that you are writing about, do not be afraid to veer off into something quite unexpected – some experience or idea that you had not even dreamed of at the start.

In spite of all his apparent fondness for the aphoristic, in the *Tractatus*, Wittgenstein claims that philosophy is not about formulating propositions. He writes: 'Philosophy does not result in "philosophical propositions", but rather in the clarification of propositions.' Philosophy, for him, is 'not a body of doctrine but an activity' (Wittgenstein 1961, 4.112).

What Wittgenstein says about philosophy can also be said of literary criticism: it is an activity. A good essay will convey a strong impression of *activity*, above all the activity of thinking critically. It will give off the scent of freshness and surprise, of discovery and the unexpected. It should not feel completely random, as if the writer really has no clue what s/he is going to say next or how one paragraph connects with another: when critical writing really works it is because the reader is led through something of the adventure in thinking out of which it emerges.

Your first draft of an essay will inevitably bear various kinds of unnecessary evidence of this adventure. It is crucial, then, to go back over it, to tweak and re-jig, revise and rewrite, rework and reshape your essay, so that it does not seem merely haphazard, arbitrary or contingent. It needs to read like a thoughtful exploration, a controlled activity, not a chaotic helter-skelter − even if that is how it came about. It needs to sound as if you know what you think − and that you really think it.

Networks and interconnections

It is important to engage with current critical thinking − with what engages, excites and challenges contemporary scholars, critics and theorists. The really interesting, really good critics are those who have learned from and elaborated on what other critics have already said. Looking at some of the most recent critical work on a given author or text is therefore invaluable. But developing and deepening an appreciation of the most influential critical thinking from the past is indispensable as well.

You might try reading some of the classics − Samuel Johnson, S.T. Coleridge, Matthew Arnold, Walter Pater, A.C. Bradley, T.S. Eliot and Virginia Woolf. They are worth reading not just for what they tell us about a particular text but also for the sharpness and originality of their critical thinking, and indeed for the quality and distinctiveness of their writing. Each of these critics provides a critical model that in turn compels our admiration and impels our critical thinking.

We want to give just one example of strong contemporary criticism in action. Maud Ellmann's *The Nets of Modernism: Henry James, Virginia Woolf, James Joyce, and Sigmund Freud* (Ellmann 2010) is an invaluable study of nets − networks and interconnections − that helps us to think about literature and culture in the early twentieth century. The second chapter of Ellmann's book is, intriguingly, provocatively, called 'The Modernist Rat', and begins as follows:

There is a legend that intertwined rats' tails can fuse together, producing a many-headed monster known as a rat-king. The largest mummified specimen of this phenomenon, whose tails are probably tied together after death, is displayed in the science museum in Altenberg, Germany. As a collective fantasy, the rat-king provides an apt analogy for the tangle of cultural anxieties represented by the rat in modernism. This chapter attempts to unravel these strands while stressing their knotted interdependence. Foremost among them is the notion of excess, whether negatively figured in the form of waste, or positively in the form of plenty. Other strands connect the atavistic to the futuristic, the savage to the citified, the bestial to the human, the mechanical to the organic, the polluted to the sterilized, the superstitious to the scientific, the foreign to the inbred, the heterogeneous to the homogenized, the chaotic to the systematic.

(Ellmann 2010, 14)

There are many reasons for seeing Ellmann's work as an excellent illustration of 'thinking critically'. To begin with, we might note the importance of surprise, a sense of freshness and the unexpected in this opening paragraph. Even the title to the chapter is striking. 'The Modernist Rat' is hardly a conventional phrase. It juxtaposes two quite different realms – a twentieth-century literary or art movement and non-human animals – in a way that might make you think, or start to think. There is an air of incongruity and intrigue: what is a 'modernist rat'? Does Ellmann mean 'rat' in some metaphorical sense? What does a *rat* have to do with 'the nets of modernism'? The chapter-title is arresting, it draws us in: we want to know what it is about, what it means.

And then the opening paragraph does not satisfy us exactly, but does something perhaps more interesting than this: Ellmann starts at a tangent, with a detail, a story ('a legend') about rats and monstrousness. If this image of the 'many-headed monster' called 'a rat-king' is strangely, disgustingly compelling in itself, it also quickly becomes clear that it is a figure or metaphor with, as it were, more twisted significance. It is interwoven with what Ellmann goes on to describe as a 'tangle of cultural anxieties' and forms of 'knotted interdependence'. Her opening paragraph is pellucid and precise. It makes deft use of literary techniques: her 'There is a legend . . .' is very close, after all, to a 'Once upon a time . . .'; and her language demonstrates a fine attunement to the power and pleasure of figurative language (the 'apt analogy', the 'tangle' of anxieties, the image of writing as a way to 'unravel these strands') and even to the sounds of words (the 'atavistic' opposing, yet almost rhyming with,

the 'futuristic', the sibilance of the 'savage' and the 'citified'). These linguistic effects are not overplayed but rich and suggestive.

At the same time, Ellmann's opening paragraph is clear and reassur-
ingly explicit in telling us what her essay is going to be about and what
'strands' in particular she proposes to explore in the pages that follow.
She wears her learning lightly: Freud is there in the book's sub-title, and
the attention here to 'collective fantasy' and 'cultural anxieties' intimates
the importance of psychoanalysis for understanding modernism and
indeed, in more general respects, for thinking critically. There may be
one or two unfamiliar words in this paragraph (the 'atavistic' or 'heterogeneous', for example), but the deployment of these terms in a series of
binary oppositions (waste / plenty, atavistic / futuristic, heterogeneous /
homogenized) makes it easy enough to infer their significance. And
while Ellmann does not specifically single out the oppositions of 'literal /
figurative' or 'reality / fantasy', the reader is invited to think about the
sense and movements of the 'rat' of the title in these respects too.

More broadly, Ellmann foregrounds two of the fundamental techniques
of critical thinking, first by nimbly moving from a detail (the story of the
rat-king) to the general, and second by illuminating the way that conceptual oppositions operate in the text. Such oppositions are everywhere –
black / white, good / evil, male / female, human / non-human animal,
body / soul, life / death. Critical thinking can often begin in thinking
critically about how oppositions work – or fail to work.

'The Modernist Rat' suggests the value of reflecting on conceptual
oppositions: to note the oppositions in a sentence or passage of writing
is a neat way of beginning to orient one's critical thinking. But the discovery or articulation of such oppositions is never sufficient in itself: it is a
matter of thinking critically *about* them, of questioning and even altering
the ways in which we think about them. It is a matter of thinking about
how such oppositions are not only in tension with, but also dependent
on, one another. This indeed, for Ellmann, is what the rat signifies.
After evoking this knotty series of oppositions (savage / citified, bestial /
human, mechanical / organic, polluted / sterilized, superstitious / scientific, etc.), she begins a new paragraph:

> The modernist rat provokes such oppositions only to confound them.
> Popping up irrepressibly in modernist texts, the rat signals the break-
> down of boundaries, at once calamitous and liberating. Traditionally
> feared as a parasite on literature, a bibliophagous menace to the
> authority of the book, the rat represents the forces of decomposition

endemic to the work of composition. As we shall see, the recurrence of the rat in modernist texts intimates that writing is riddled with erasure, and that literature is a self-gnawing artefact.

(Ellmann 2010, 14)

This is agile, energetic writing. (We would say 'rat-like', but that might give the wrong impression.) Ellmann advances here, then, on what she set up in the preceding paragraph. It is now evident that we are being presented with nothing less than a re-thinking of modernist literature in terms of the figure of the rat. The rat chews through the oppositions Ellmann had earlier established.

In language that is lucid, playful and inventive (the rat 'popping up', literature as 'self-gnawing', the 'bibliophagous'), Ellmann's writing conveys an exciting mixture of adventure and control. As we might hope from the opening page of a critical essay, the author gives us a clear sense of where her thinking has led her, of where the essay is going to take us. This is especially evident in her use of prolepsis, the rhetorical device by which she tells the reader what lies ahead: 'This chapter attempts . . .' (in the first paragraph); and 'As we shall see . . .' (in the second).

As a 'parasite', as a figure that overturns or 'confound[s]' oppositions, the rat has a menacing and disruptive character. It 'signals the breakdown of boundaries'. The rat alerts us to the ways in which literature is 'riddled with erasure': the literary work always has bits missing, things unspoken, gaps or silences that are crucial to how we read. Ellmann's opening paragraph gives a powerful sense of *activity* (to recall Wittgenstein's word): it is not just the rat, but her own writing that gives us a sharp impression that it is *at work*. It is active, up to stuff, doing things with words.

Maud Ellmann's study of nets and networks, connections and dependencies, is exemplary of broader developments in critical thinking and the humanities. Timothy Morton names this phenomenon 'the ecological thought': in his book of that title he spells out the ways in which 'the *ecological thought* is the thinking of interconnectedness' (Morton 2010, 7). Henry James's remark (in 1907) that 'Really . . . relations stop nowhere' (quoted in Ellmann 2010, 1) has taken on a new, unprecedented critical force. Thinking critically involves close reading – a careful attention to a specific text and, more narrowly, what is going on in a particular paragraph or sentence, even a certain word or phrase – but it also requires us to focus on interconnectedness. We live in a networked world, that is to say in a world in which we confront urgent questions of justice and inequality, democracy and worldwide human rights, climate change and ecological transformation. Engaging with these questions is a pressing and fundamental part of what 'thinking critically' means.

Summary

The opening paragraphs of Ellmann's essay suggest that thinking and writing critically should entail (so to speak) being attentive to some of the following:

- **Connections, tensions and oppositions** – some of which may be odd or surprising.
- **Historical context** – in this case, early twentieth-century Europe and North America.
- **The strange nature of literary language** – the significance and effects of rhetorical figures and tropes, such as storytelling, metaphorical language and so on.
- **The dynamic possibilities of writing** itself as an act or activity, a critical and creative putting into action of 'how to do things with words' (Austin 1962).

Further reading

On critical thinking and criticism in general, Marjorie Garber's *A Manifesto for Literary Studies* (2003) is a good, polemical place to start. Rather differently, *The Johns Hopkins Guide to Literary Theory and Criticism* (Groden and Kreiswirth 2005) is a useful reference work, as is the multi-volume *Cambridge History of Literary Criticism* (9 vols, 1990–2013) which contains a wealth of material on the history of the discipline. Thinking has, for at least a couple of millennia, tended to be associated with philosophy. Besides Wittgenstein's *Philosophical Investigations* (especially paragraphs 327–390), you might also like to explore the writings of Martin Heidegger in this context, including *What Is Called Thinking?* (1968), *Early Greek Thinking* (1976) and *Poetry, Language, Thought* (1975). But it is hardly the case that poets, novelists and dramatists have shown no interest in this topic. If you carry out a quick search of appearances of 'think' (and its cognates) in, say, Shakespeare's plays, the poetry of Wordsworth or the novels of Samuel Beckett, you will soon find yourself in fascinating places. Especially in the context of poetry, see the special issue of *Textual Practice* entitled *Thinking Poetry* (2010), ed. Peter Boxall, which includes J.H. Prynne's compact but compelling essay, 'Poetic Thought'. For a provoking exploration of the relation between thinking and environmentalism, see Timothy Morton's *The Ecological Thought* (2010). For a brilliant discussion of what it might mean to talk about a 'university of Thought', see Bill Readings' *The University in Ruins* (1996). In *Professing Criticism* (2022), John Guillory offers a bracing and powerful diagnosis of the field of literary criticism and of critical thinking as such; while in a special issue of *Textual Practice* on 'The Future of Literary Thinking' (2016), thirty critics provide their succinct and thought-provoking speculations on the topic. Finally, on aphorism, see Ben Grant's useful and fittingly succinct book *The Aphorism and Other Short Forms* (2016) and Noreen Masud's brilliant book on Stevie Smith and on so much more, *Stevie Smith and the Aphorism: Hard Language* (2023).

Part III
Writing

9.   Writing an essay

Rather than writing an essay on how to write an essay, which sounds like an oddly circular enterprise, we propose instead to offer a series of fuses that might help ignite your essay or reignite your thoughts once you have written a draft of it.

You need help

We do not mean this in a medical or psychiatric sense. We are not recommending the use of pharmaceutical substances to enhance your performance. But one of the first things to realize is that writing a good essay involves making use of what others have said and thought. There is sometimes a tendency to suppose that you need to be original, to push others to one side, in order to have 'your own voice'. 'Originality' is, after all, one of the usual criteria for an excellent essay or dissertation.

But originality (if there is such a thing) does not come from cutting yourself off and imagining you can work alone, like a solitary genius without books on a desert island. In the words of Ian Dury and the Blockheads, 'There ain't half been some clever bastards'. If you want to write good essays, read some of the classics, by critics such as Samuel Johnson, William Hazlitt, Ralph Waldo Emerson, Matthew Arnold, John Ruskin, Walter Pater, T.S. Eliot, Virginia Woolf and Lionel Trilling. Brilliant, compelling, often wonderfully perceptive but also on occasion woefully wrong, they all have a great deal to give, both in terms of literary knowledge and insight and in terms of the art of essay writing.

Have a look at the work of perhaps the most remarkable essay-writer who ever lived, Michel de Montaigne (1533–92). One of the

DOI: 10.4324/9781003301363-12

most immediately striking features of Montaigne's essays is how consistently they draw on other writers and thinkers. They are packed with quotations from what others have said and thought. Montaigne himself reflects on this process, in his essay 'On Educating Children':

> Bees ransack flowers here and flowers there: but then they make their own honey, which is entirely theirs and no longer thyme or marjoram. Similarly the boy will transform his borrowings; he will confound their forms so that the end-product is entirely his: namely, his judgement, the forming of which is the only aim of his toil, his study and his education.
>
> (Montaigne 2003, 171)

Montaigne is not making a plea for plagiarism but rather suggesting that a distinctive poetic or critical voice is inevitably composed of the thoughts, arguments and inspiration of others. For the essay-writer it is imperative to acknowledge clearly what is being borrowed or cited, whether it is the particular words and phrases, or just the ideas or line of argument, of another critic. But the way in which you make use of what others have said and thought can be 'entirely [your own]'. Writers are bees, quotations are flowers and the essay is honey. Montaigne implies here that the primary purpose of education is to become truly critical – to read, think and write critically. For a twentieth-century formulation of this idea, we might ransack T.S. Eliot's essay 'Philip Massinger' (1920), in which he contends that 'Immature poets imitate; mature poets steal; bad poets deface what they take, and good poets make it into something better, or at least something different' (Eliot 1975, 153).

Take notes as you read

It is crucial to annotate as you go. Intriguing, striking or wonderful as you might find an image or phrase or passage in Jane Austen or Ralph Ellison, in Edmund Spenser or August Strindberg, you just won't remember effectively without making a note of it. If it is your own book, make pencil notes in the margins or at the back, or you can keep a running list going on a separate piece of paper. Marking up your text makes it simple to locate those moments that you consider of particular interest or importance: an especially striking description of place or character, a significant revelation or turn in the unfolding of the plot, something you find notably sad, funny, imaginative, moving or strange. It might be the phrasing of a sentence or passage, or indeed just a single word that strikes you as interesting or notable. You may also find it helpful to keep track of particular recurrent features, such as the repetition of certain words or images or the insistence of certain themes or ideas. Think of your annotations as your own personal index to the book you are reading. You can return to your annotations when it comes to essay writing time: they are there to remind you of what you found exciting, intriguing, brilliant and so on. They speed up the process of re-establishing your overall impression of the book and help you clarify what you might want to say about it.

Write a letter

People are always writing, sending or receiving letters in literature. So-called 'epistolary novels', for example, are explicitly in the form of a series of letters, and poems are often, if only implicitly, in the form of some kind of letter. (Almost all of the eighty-eight poems in Ted Hughes's *Birthday Letters* (1998) are addressed to Sylvia Plath, for instance, while her poem 'Daddy' (1962) is addressed, like a letter, to her dead father.) When E.M. Forster gives advice on novel-writing, he says: 'Not a bad plan to think a novel's going to be a letter' (Forster 1976, 162). Not a bad plan, either, to think of your essay as a kind of letter – but with a clear introduction, middle and conclusion. Thinking of your essay as a letter helps you to keep in mind the importance of the reader, and of writing in a lucid and appealing way. Montaigne's essay 'On Educating Children' was itself originally written as a letter to Madame Diane de Foix regarding the education of her young son.

Answer the question (and keep answering it)

Sometimes you might have an essay in which the question has been specified in advance; at other times you may be expected to devise your own essay question. Whichever it is, you need to *answer the question*. In your first paragraph you should briefly make it clear, first and foremost, *how* you are going to be answering the question. (Sounds a bit obvious, doesn't it? But it is remarkable how many essay-openings fail to do it.) Of course, 'answering the question' in literary studies is often far from straightforward. In a sense – as we have been trying to make clear throughout this book – literature only ever answers questions with more questions (or with silence). That is what makes literary texts so endlessly fascinating, compelling, exasperating, enigmatic, exhilarating and liberating to write about. In your essay, you should try to do justice to the uncertainties and ambiguities, to the *questioning power* of the text you are studying, as well as to provide an articulate response to the specific question or topic you are addressing.

Say 'I'

Some people seem to think that there is a veto or taboo regarding the use of the first person singular in academic writing. (Admittedly we never do it, but that is because there are two of us: our book is written in the 'Bennett-and-Royle we'.) Following such a veto or taboo can turn the essay into an awkward exercise in self-defence, pervaded by impersonal and non-idiomatic formulations such as 'In the essay it will be argued that . . .', 'Having focused on . . . the essay will now . . .', 'In the preceding pages it has been demonstrated . . .' and so on. We hereby confirm that there is nothing at all wrong with using 'I' in your essay writing. The only thing you need to ensure is that you deploy your 'I' in a critical and judicious way. By this we mean that you need to convince people. As in so much else, in essay writing as in so-called real life, balance is crucial. You don't want to overdo it: 'I' this, 'I' that, 'I' the next thing, over and over again, like any other repeated formulation, tends to become dreary. Occasional use of a more objective-sounding form ('It may be helpful to . . .'), the passive ('Particular attention will be given to . . .') or indeed a first person plural form ('As we have seen . . .') creates a greater sense of variety, depth and linguistic assurance.

Set things up in your opening

The opening paragraph or two should not only make it transparent and obvious that you are going to be answering the question but should also make it clear *how, why* and *with what consequences*. In your introduction, in other words, you should indicate in a direct and straightforward fashion what the question involves, what complexities or challenges it entails, and how you propose to go about dealing with these issues. A strong essay will often also explicitly acknowledge and say something in its opening paragraph about the singularity and power of the literary work itself. Bear in mind that, however long your essay is supposed to be, you are never going to be able to say everything there is to say about the text/s or writer/s you are discussing. A good essay, then, tends to establish its parameters in the opening paragraph: it describes and defines its territory and often tries to indicate at the outset what will be excluded.

Connect your middle bits

Your middle paragraphs need to follow a clear path towards the conclusion that you will already have indicated in your introduction. You probably won't know exactly what your conclusion is while you are writing the first draft of your essay. (Don't worry: this is perfectly normal, as a doctor might say.) But when you are producing your final version of the essay, it needs to be evident where you are going as you go. You should not treat your reader as a simpleton, but you should clearly signal what is happening from one paragraph to the next in terms of the development of your response to the question. If you are looking for a way of getting structure into your middle paragraphs, draw up a list of the quotations you find most obviously relevant, as well as (from your own point of view as a reader) most rich and illuminating for your topic. There is no hard-and-fast rule about this, of course, but for a 2,000-word essay this might mean half a dozen quotations, of varying length; twelve or fifteen quotations for a 4,000-word essay; and so on. These quotations can operate as goals or focal points to drive your argument forward from one paragraph to the next. Always bear in mind the importance of close reading: spending time trying to do justice to a particular word, line or passage from the text under consideration is crucial to a good essay. But remember, too, that close reading needs to be relevant: you need to relate your reading of the quoted passage to the essay topic.

Your concluding paragraph should worry you

The problem with conclusions is that they can be a bit boring, since they tend to make it explicit that you have done what you said you were going to do in your opening paragraph. An arresting ending usually involves at least two ingredients: (1) it performs a sort of valedictory handshake with the essay question: recapping on how the question has indeed been the subject of the preceding pages; (2) it does not simply feel like box-ticking: think of putting an extra squeeze into that handshake, add a final clinching quotation and critical comment and / or identify some way in which, given the opportunity, the topic might be explored further or in slightly different ways. In order to remain loyal to the principle of close reading and to a sense of respect for the richness and complexity of the text you have been writing about, it is often neat to end with something from the text under consideration (perhaps something concerned with how it ends).

Get close, but go far

Quotation and close reading are crucial. Quotations make an essay's world go round. But at the same time do not forget about breadth. Your essay might require you to focus in detail on a play by Harold Pinter, but do not be afraid to draw briefly on your knowledge of, say, Beckett or Shakespeare when commenting on a Pinter quotation. You will invariably be admired for wearing your knowledge lightly while nevertheless showing that you have in fact read *Waiting for Godot* or *King Lear* and realized that it has a specific resonance or connection with what Pinter's play is up to.

What if you are asked to devise your own question?

If you are expected to work out your own essay topic, make sure you word it clearly and simply. Do not set yourself a question that encourages a straightforward 'Yes' or 'No' or 'Not really' answer. Think of a question or statement that is provoking and intriguing but that also gives you room for manoeuvre – an opportunity to take the topic and run with it somewhere that you will find interesting and rewarding.

Remember that an essay title does not need to be in the form of an explicit question, and it is often best if it is short and snappy, rather than wordy and overly explanatory. An essay-title such as, say, 'Waste in T.S. Eliot's *The Waste Land*' or 'Beckett's "Molloy" and the Labour of Writing' can work quite well. On the other hand, it is often helpful to have a question or essay-title that involves reacting to (or starting out from) a quotation, either from the author about whose work you are supposed to be writing or from a critic (who may be named or may be anonymous and indeed even imaginary). You might consider quoting a sentence, a phrase or just a word or two from, say, Keats or Woolf or Joyce, then inserting a colon, and following this with the topic and author / text. For example:

> ' "To cease upon the midnight with no pain": Death in Keats's Poetry'
> ' "Yes, of course, if it's fine tomorrow": Write an essay on affirmation in Woolf's *To the Lighthouse*'

'"What birds were they?": Figures of Flight in Joyce's *A Portrait of the Artist as a Young Man*'.

Alternatively, you might use a succinct sentence, phrase or just a word or two by another critic to set up your chosen topic. Whichever way you do it, try to make the title punchy and intriguing – something interesting to yourself but also inviting to your reader.

Act like a lawyer

When it comes to essay writing, there are numerous parallels and similarities between a literary critic writing an essay and a lawyer in a court-case. An essay is a kind of trial, not just in the funny sense of being trying. The word 'essay', after all, is from the old French verb *essayer*, to try or to examine, and people still use (if a little comically or pompously) the verb 'essay' (or 'assay'). With an essay, as with a trial in court, there is always an element of the unpredictable. Nothing is assured in advance.

As a lawyer, it may seem to you a no-brainer that the woman poisoned her husband because he couldn't find the winning lottery ticket, but you still have to make a case and persuade the jury. In the same way, an essay involves making a case and persuading your reader. What is your case? Outline the case in your opening paragraph. Then in the subsequent paragraphs, make your case and persuade your reader. Just as, in a trial scene, the lawyer needs evidence, so in your essay you need to offer evidence for what you are saying. The lawyer will provide evidence of the fact that the man was poisoned, that there really was a lottery ticket and so on; in your case, *the evidence is the text*. You need to supply precise textual corroboration to support and substantiate what you are saying. Where appropriate you may want to bring in further witnesses (another critic or critics) who back up your view. But the real evidence is the text itself. And, as a rule of thumb, you should never make an assertion without providing evidence.

It is not enough, however, simply to quote the text. This would be like the lawyer simply holding up a dark brown bottle and not explaining what it is or where it comes from or why it matters. You need to make it clear *why* you have quoted the phrase or line or passage that you have quoted. How does this quotation illustrate or substantiate your point? Comment, describe, question, analyse and elucidate.

Remember also, however, that a good lawyer not only knows how to be plain and direct but also likes to surprise the court. If you have a really lovely bit of evidence, think about how and when you want to introduce it in order to produce a strong effect. Sometimes you may want to hold back certain details, or conversely, you might want to dangle a certain item in front of your reader as a way of saying: I shall explain this later.

Always bear in mind the importance and power of persuasion. Nice turns of phrase, resonant or memorable ways of expressing an idea, the occasional unexpected metaphor or vivid use of an everyday idiom: these are all potentially valuable effects. But don't strain to be clever or complicated for the sake of it. Remember what Montaigne says in his essay on education: 'When eloquence draws attention to itself it does wrong' (Montaigne 2003, 194).

Simple is elegant

Don't be afraid to experiment

Remember that the word 'essay', like 'trial', has to do with experimenting. The final version of your essay needs to read *as if you knew in advance* what it was you wanted to write about and as if you knew how you were going to go about it. But everyone knows that that is not what writing is like. It is not how people actually proceed when they write a first draft.

Writing is discovering

When writing is going well, it is not necessarily because you are 'in control' of where it is going. On the contrary, it is often because you have, in some sense, let go: you have let the writing take you wherever it is going. A remark by the poet Geoffrey Hill captures this nicely: 'I write / to astonish myself' (Hill 2002, 23). Of course, it is very often the case, if you are writing an essay in literary studies, that you are led on not so much by your own words as by the words of the writer whose work you are discussing. Some of the most pleasurable and exciting moments in writing come when you have quoted something and then start to discover things about the quotation (and connections with other quotations or other observations in your essay) as you are in the very process of writing.

Write early

You don't need to wait until you have read everything there is to read on the topic you want to write about. (This is in any case impossible: there is, strictly speaking, no end to reading, no limit to 'establishing a context'.) Reading around the subject and taking notes is an important part of the process, but you don't need to be entirely clear about the focus of your essay when you start writing. Researching your topic and writing should not be seen as completely separate activities, but can often proceed simultaneously or in overlapping fashion.

What are you saying?

Ask yourself this question. Try to come up with an answer in the form of a single sentence. (And not a really long sentence: keep it as clear and simple as possible.) This is your 'thesis statement', as it is sometimes called. You can ask yourself this before you start your reading and preparation for the essay: 'What am I going to say?' or 'What do I think I am going to say?' or 'What do I think I would like to say?' It is quite probable that you do not have the faintest idea. After all, you have not yet begun reading and researching. But it is still, we think, helpful to do it, because it becomes absolutely crucial in the later stages of composition.

Ask the question again at the point when you have completed a first draft. And then ask yourself again (if you still have not managed to compose a single-sentence response) when you have a second or third or final draft. A good essay can *always* be summed up in terms of a single sentence. Think of your reader or examiner, who may have dozens of essays to grade: s/he will probably jot down somewhere in his or her notes what your essay is about. If the examiner can encapsulate your essay in a sentence, so can you.

Coming up with that sentence is a bit like finding gold. Having a pithy single-sentence version of what your essay is about will then provide you with a way of refashioning or otherwise revising your draft so that it becomes quite clear and straightforward how each of your paragraphs relates to this core sentence or idea. Every paragraph, in other words, should contain traces of that gold.

Your opening sentence might be your undoing

There is an odd little book called *The Exam Secret* by a man called Dennis Jackson, first published in 1954 but still in print. No doubt a principal reason for its popularity is the word 'secret' in its title. But Jackson's book is hopelessly out of date in all sorts of ways and we would not recommend it as a guide, let alone as the godsend its title might appear to promise. But at the heart of *The Exam Secret* is a very canny and, we think, valuable bit of advice, namely to *start your essay with a strong opening sentence*. Make sure it is clear and, if possible, refreshing and distinctive. Then try to make sure the same is true of your second sentence, and your third and so on.

We would like to offer you our own exam secret: your examiner is a tired and probably rather irritable person who is looking out for a reason *not to read* or, at least, who is in danger of thinking your essay is just a continuation of the same old same old (i.e. the essay s/he was reading before s/he picked up yours). The truth is that the reader's judgement of the quality of your essay may be quite heavily influenced by your opening sentence and, beyond that, your opening paragraph.

While Bennett and Royle have never encountered such a thing closer to home, they have been reliably informed of a case, at a prestigious university on the eastern seaboard of the United States, of a student in geology who submitted a fifteen-page essay and received a perfectly respectable grade for his work: the first couple of pages and the last couple of pages were written as a standard sort of response on the topic, the eleven or twelve pages in the middle simply ran: 'rocks, rocks, rocks, rocks, rocks, rocks, rocks, rocks, rocks, rocks, rocks, rocks . . .'.

If in doubt, cut it out

Nowadays most people write their essays on a computer. It is a doddle compared with how it used to be, when an essay had to be written by hand, then revised and written or typed out afresh. But the ease of writing, cutting and pasting on a screen comes with difficulties of another kind. In particular, writing onto a computer screen seems to encourage a sort of glazen-eyed sense that everything is okay and everything is more or less worth keeping. You might bear in mind the inverse of this idea. It is neatly captured, once again, in a brief but pointed remark from Montaigne: 'The world is nothing but chatter: I have never met a man who does not say more than he should rather than less. Yet half of our life is spent on that' (Montaigne 2003, 189).

A good essay is a work of concision, economy and compactness, and you should fully expect that there will be bits (sometimes quite good or interesting bits) that do not make it to the final draft. Always keep your eye on the main chance, in other words the importance of answering the question, developing your response, sticking to the topic. It is helpful to have a separate document for supplementary material when you are working on your essay, another file into which you can drop anything that you are not quite sure about.

If you need further encouragement on this front, think of the incisive words of the contemporary French writer and critic Hélène Cixous, in her essay 'Writing Blind':

> Breaking. Cutting. Letting go. Cutting is an art I have acquired. Nothing is more natural and more necessary. All living beings, mammal or vegetable, know that one must cut and trim to relaunch life. Nip the quick. Harm to help.
>
> (Cixous 1998, 144)

Every sentence counts

You should proceed on the basis that every sentence is significant and should add something to your account. Every sentence should have sharpness and clarity. One of the unfortunate consequences of writing on a computer screen is that people very often do not think ahead to the end of the sentence but go on (as in the case, alas, of the present sentence) writing in the hope that, in the end, it will all come around and, with luck, show itself to have been worthwhile as a further contribution, however minimal, to the essay topic that has been assigned. The previous sentence is a case in point: it is long and unwieldy, repetitious and awkward. Writing on a computer seems to encourage this tendency.

When you revise, look out for over-long sentence-structures. If you see one, sort it out. Either rework it into two sentences or find a way of breaking it up: sometimes (as here) you can do it with a colon. (Be wary of the semi-colon; it is no substitute for a well-placed comma, colon or full stop. 'How hideous is the semi-colon', as Samuel Beckett's *Watt* has it (Beckett 2009, 135). Only rarely is it useful, for example in the compilation of a lengthy or complex list.) This is not to say that long sentences are innately bad. We ourselves, you may have noticed, are not averse to the occasional extended sentence-structure. But we also like a pithy sentence. Check it out. Deliberately varying the length of your sentences has several potential benefits:

(1) it tends to be more enjoyable, unpredictable or surprising for your reader;
(2) it brings rhythm (a sense of voice) more sharply into the body of your writing;

(3) it is a way of learning more about how language works, about what words can do and how syntax (the word-order and structure of a sentence) can affect or indeed entirely alter what you are saying.

Silly as it may sound, reading your essay out loud is one of the most effective ways of tidying or tightening up your writing. Do it, if you can, with a friend or even, if needs be, your dog or, perhaps, your friend's dog. Hearing your sentences as you read them aloud can be the quickest way of discovering whether or not they work. Are you satisfied with each sentence? Is it comfortable, even pleasurable, to read out loud? Could this or that sentence be somehow honed or otherwise sharpened up? Do it. And remember our motto: if in doubt, cut it out.

Quote or perish

Remember this rough rule of thumb: your comment on a quotation should be about as long as what you have quoted. If you quote ten lines from D.H. Lawrence, you should expect to spend ten lines commenting on it. (Of course, should you become fascinated with a single sentence, or with a single line of poetry, don't be surprised if you have to break the rule because you have so much you want to say.) Try to do the quotation justice: why have you chosen it? What is especially interesting, relevant, strange, thought-provoking, elegant or perhaps beautiful about it? Describe this.

Once you have a first draft of your essay, stop!

Have a cup of tea, go for a run or watch a movie (or even all three, though perhaps not at the same time): 'unwind yourself', as King Louie in Disney's *Jungle Book* puts it. You need to forget – or at least put at a distance – what it was you were doing. Most people will have had the strange experience of coming across something they wrote in the past (it might be a diary, a letter or just an email) and thinking: 'Did I write that? Weird!' Getting some distance on the essay that you are writing is essential. You can then return to it with a slightly different eye and ear and read it a little more as if you were a stranger, rather than its anxious, possessive creator. It is a matter of trying to read as if you do not already know – as if you have truly forgotten – what you have said and why. And then keep asking yourself: 'Have I said what I mean? Have I put it as clearly as I can?'

Keep revising

Make sure you revise your work more than once. Much of what we have said has to do with this process of revision, which should be seen as an integral part of essay writing rather than as a bolt-on that you will do if you have the time or if you can be bothered. Sometimes the most interesting or exciting discoveries about your essay come only as you are revising it for what you expect or fear or hope will be the last time. Late additions or modifications can crucially clarify, enhance and sharpen your argument. Conversely, you might also see, at the very end, pleasing ways in which you can omit and tighten.

Have you finished?

Look over your essay and ask yourself: is it absolutely clear that I have answered the question? Is it absolutely clear that this is the case in the very first paragraph and also in the final paragraph? Is it clear how each of the paragraphs in between the introduction and conclusion constitutes an explicit development of my response to the question? Is it clear how each paragraph follows on from the last and leads on to the next? If the answer to any of these questions is 'no' or 'dunno', you need to go back to the relevant paragraph and revise it in such a way that it becomes absolutely clear *how* it relates to the essay question or essay topic. If you cannot see how it relates, or how to make it relate, then you need to delete the paragraph.

Enjoy yourself, if you possibly can

A good essay gives pleasure. When you enjoy writing about the text/s or writer/s you are focusing on in your essay, this is likely to be something your reader comes to share. Thinking may be hard, expressing and structuring your ideas may be challenging and even frustrating (is anyone ever entirely satisfied with an essay they have written?), but your writing should also convey a sense of the exhilaration and playfulness of language, as well as the love of words, evident in all great works of literature.

Further reading

David Kennedy's online Royal Literary Fund *Essay Guide* at: www.rlf. org.uk/fellowshipscheme/writing/essayguide.cfm provides lots of good practical advice. Fabb and Durant's *How to Write Essays and Dissertations*

(2005) is another excellent guide. On issues of spelling, punctuation and grammar, in particular, we would recommend Peck and Coyle's *The Student's Guide to Writing: Spelling, Punctuation and Grammar* (2012). For a sense of the richness of the art of essay writing, perhaps the obvious place to start is the work of Montaigne. The best and fullest English version is *The Complete Essays*, translated by M.A. Screech (2003). For a dense but remarkable series of reflections on the importance and potential of 'the essay as form', see Adorno's essay of that title. Another indispensable writer in this context is Walter Benjamin. The essays collected in *Illuminations*, for example, include such brilliant and influential pieces as 'The Storyteller' and 'The Work of Art in the Age of Mechanical Reproduction'. On the relation between essay writing and the unforeseeable, see Hélène Cixous's extraordinary little text, 'Writing Blind'. We also recommend Elena Ferrante's *In the Margins* (2022): although not explicitly focused on essay writing, her book is a wonderful example of essayistic thinking.

10. Creative writing

The impossible

The expansion of creative writing courses has been one of the most dramatic developments in the recent history of 'English' as a discipline. In the following pages, we move on to questions about how to think about 'creative writing' – about what exactly it is, how it relates to studying literature and why it might matter. In the chapter after this, we talk about how you might go about actually producing some creative writing (specifically a work of short fiction). Even if you are not interested in pursuing creative writing yourself, we hope that these pages might help to clarify the ways in which it has, for better or worse, changed the nature of literary studies. If climate change is the term for what is happening to the world's weather, creative writing has been producing 'discipline change' in literary studies.

One of the longstanding questions lurking around the topic of creative writing is 'Can it be taught?' or 'How do you learn it?' In our view, teaching creative writing is impossible. But this need not mean that it is not worth trying, or that valuable and productive things cannot flow from the attempt. Sigmund Freud says that there are three impossible professions: government, psychoanalysis and teaching (see Freud 2002, 203). If teaching is an impossible profession, what difference does 'creative writing' make to the mix? Might it not help us think more clearly and come up with more inventive ideas for education more generally?

People talk about 'mission impossible' or being in an 'impossible situation', but what is the impossible, in truth? An initial thought might be that lots of things are impossible: travelling back in time; travelling forward in time; knowing what happens when you die or returning from the dead; inhabiting someone else's mind, thoughts and feelings;

DOI: 10.4324/9781003301363-13

discovering overnight that you have turned into an enormous insect. All of these examples are drawn from literature and offer indeed a sort of condensed illustration of what literature is. Creative writing (whether poetry, fiction, drama or creative non-fiction) is the space in which these impossible things can occur. Here are some examples:

1. **Time-travel is possible.** Not just H.G. Wells's *The Time Machine*, but every work of fiction, and perhaps even every poem and play, every memoir or autobiography invites us to construe it – and join in with it – as an experience of time-travel. Literary texts can transport us across decades or lifetimes, pitch us into the future or drag us back in time.

2. **The dead can return.** Not just in Shakespeare's *Hamlet* or Emily Brontë's *Wuthering Heights* or Don DeLillo's *The Body Artist*, but all literary works are made of voices and words that come to us from the dead. All literary works have to do with forms of cultural memory that stretch back from before we were born, with senses of loss and ghostly repetitions or revivals. Sooner or later all authors will be dead and are indeed, in a spooky but telling sense, already dead, insofar as their texts have a capacity to live on after them.

3. **Inhabiting someone else's mind happens all the time in literature.** Sometimes matter-of-factly, sometimes comically, sometimes uncannily, literature is where the hidden world of what others are thinking and feeling is revealed. It is where what philosophers refer to as 'the problem of other minds' is temporarily, strangely, impossibly solved.

4. **You can find yourself transformed into a gigantic insect.** This is what happens in Kafka's story 'The Metamorphosis', but metamorphosis – whereby one person or creature changes into some other person or creature, into someone else, or into some *thing* else – is far more widely present in works of literature than you might think. Indeed, one of the most influential works in Western literature is Ovid's *Metamorphoses*, a poem in Latin that recounts the history of the world through a series of stories about transformations or metamorphoses of the human, animal or divine that have given rise to the modern (Roman) world. Poets, in particular, have a striking tendency to identify with, or project themselves into non-human animals or objects. We might think, for instance, of George Herbert's 'Affliction (I)' in which the poet laments: 'I reade, and sigh, and wish I were a tree' (Herbert 2007, 163), or Ted Hughes's

'Hawk Roosting', in which the 'I' sits in 'the top of the wood' and 'in sleep rehearse[s] perfect kills and eat[s]' (Hughes 2003, 68–69). Fiction-writers and dramatists, in particular, have a constitutional commitment to turning themselves into other people. (Even if those other people bear a marked resemblance to themselves – as in Charlotte Brontë's *Villette*, James Joyce's *A Portrait of the Artist as a Young Man*, Saul Bellow's *Herzog* or Leila Aboulela's *The Translator*.) That is their job, in a nutshell, the first line of their job description: *Become some other person or creature.* Neither the first-person narrator nor any of the characters in a work of fiction is simply identical with the author. Only the most naive, uncritical readers or spectators would take it into their head that the protagonist or other character in a play is actually the playwright. Luigi Pirandello makes the comic naivety of this kind of thinking explicit in *Six Characters in Search of an Author* (1921). It is a wonderfully chaotic staging of characters (Mother, Father, Stepdaughter and so on) and the actors who are supposed to 'be' or 'become' them, together with 'the producer' – all of whom are *in search of an author* (an author who does not appear on stage but is said to sit 'in his gloomy study', as 'shadows . . . fill the room', refusing to grant 'life' to his characters (Pirandello 1985, 124–125)). Forms of metamorphosis may be discerned in every poem or play or work of fiction – even, or perhaps above all, in the way that the author disappears into his or her text.

In all of these instances, then, we could say that creative writing has a remarkable, even unique significance in relation to thinking about the impossible. Doubtless we are drawn to reading literary works (just as we may also be drawn to watching movies or gaming) because they enable us, in some sense, to depart from reality and enter impossible worlds. But creative writing is different because it is concerned not just with creating those worlds oneself but, in principle at least, with preserving them in writing for others. The pursuit of creative writing, the creative writing workshop, the phenomenon of creative writing as a part of literary studies – all of these have to do with you personally, on your own. You, with just your pen and piece of paper, or blank computer screen, negotiating the impossible *in the present*.

There is something rather terrifying about this scenario. (It's no wonder that people talk about 'writer's block'.) And in that sense, we might ask whose bright idea it was to introduce such an unnerving situation into the university classroom. Of course, the fact that you are in a building for educational purposes, that a tutor or lecturer is present in the room, the fact that what you are doing, or supposed to be doing, is ultimately connected to some form of assessment and so on, all help to convey a sense that you can, and should, 'keep calm and carry on'. But in truth there is something quite mad about a creative writing class. King Lear's frenzied words, 'O that way madness lies; let me shun that; / No more of that' (3.4.21–22), might readily echo down the centuries into the silence of your mind as you sit in that classroom faced with the task of writing something now, this very minute – something that will constitute an encounter with the impossible and prove worthy of the name 'creative writing'.

Indeed, far from wanting to offer a comforting or anodyne, merely 'institutionalized' conception of creative writing here, we would like to stress that it is a potentially disruptive and innovative activity – not only for oneself but also for the institution in which it takes place. It may be fruitful and transformative in ways that go beyond the individual concerns of the creative writing student. And this can come about, we suggest, through explicit critical reflection on what 'creative writing' is or might be. There is no truly creative writing without critical thinking – including thinking about the purpose and value of the university, and about how creative writing addresses and engages with social, ethical and other worldly and environmental issues beyond the university.

At this point we might recall those three impossible professions to which Freud referred – government, psychoanalysis and teaching itself – and say something about creative writing's role in relation to each of them.

Government

To reflect critically on creative writing inevitably entails an engagement with the nature of authority and control – with questions of 'self-control', hence 'self-government', as well as 'whose words are these that I am writing?', 'is my language my own?', 'according to whose authority, how and why, am I going to be judged and assessed?', 'what is authority, anyway?' and so on. You don't have to suffer from paranoid delusions of being watched by the government to realize that 'creative writing' ('go on, be creative, write something creative!') confronts you with yourself, with fundamental questions not just about who you think you are, but about what drives you, about who or what is guiding, managing, constraining but also perhaps liberating what you are writing or what you dream of writing.

To pursue creative writing in a thoughtful and critical manner is necessarily to engage with broader questions: about self and community, about the value and purpose of working with others, about the relations between the creative writing classroom and the world, writing and what is sometimes called the 'real'. Who knows what is going to come into your head next or where it will have come from? What distinguishes creative writing from other university subjects is that it pivots on a specific crisis of the present. Poised in the now, the writer is immersed in a certain experience of anarchy. This moment is governed, if it is governed at all, by a sense of promise, a dream of the future. And this sense of promise or dream is not simply about *you* but about the fact that a creative writing class or workshop is a group event. The reason you have chosen to study or take a course in creative writing has something to do with the nature of being and working with others, of reliance on others. It is about you, but not all about you.

Psychoanalysis

More than any other area of literary studies, creative writing conducts you to a strange interior world. In this it has strong affinities with psychoanalysis. Unlike studying, say, the Romantic lyric, or the postmodern novel, you have no model or example on which to focus. Rather, it is all in your head. As we have been intimating, madness is, if you think about it, never far away. The 'space of composition', as Timothy Clark has described it, presents a crisis of subjectivity (Clark 1997, 22). More than anything else studied in the humanities, creative writing invites you to look within, to reflect on who or what you are, on what you desire, on how you think and on how your desires and thinking might be most effectively realized in words. But let us say it again: it is not all about you. At least it is not necessarily about a 'you' that you would recognize.

This idea calls for some further elucidation. Like psychoanalysis, creative writing is profoundly concerned not only with the nature of language and the self, but also with what Havelock Ellis called 'the world of dreams' (Ellis 1911). Freud once wrote a little essay about 'Creative Writers and Day-Dreaming' (1908) – an essay that writers often refer to in a sniffy or dismissive way, on the basis that the founder of psychoanalysis characterizes creative writing in an overly simple and reductive fashion. In particular, Freud seeks to categorize creative writing as more or less equivalent to daydreaming. The creative writer by this account emerges as a complacent, egocentric person inspired only by a desire to fulfil their fantasies in writing. In the process, Freud deliberately restricts himself to 'the less pretentious authors of novels, romances and short stories, who nevertheless have the widest and most eager circle of readers of both sexes' (Freud 1985, 137). Reading Freud's essay today, it is difficult not to think about how much we would need to modify or rework what he says in order to try to take into account more complex kinds of creative writing. What if Freud had focused his attention not on a simple 'daydream' model but on the work of Shakespeare, for example, or Dostoevsky? Literary works such as Shakespeare's *A Midsummer Night's Dream* or Dostoevsky's *The Double* are not just dreams or daydreams but have a reflexive or analytic dimension of their own – they are *about* dreaming, they refer to themselves as fictions, they have in some ways as much to tell us about psychoanalysis, as psychoanalysis might have to tell us about them.

At the same time, we should not lose sight of the fact that 'Creative Writers and Day-Dreaming' is a little masterpiece of sorts. It calls for what we have described as creative reading. It contains numerous brilliant insights and observations about the nature of creative writing while also exhibiting something of the dreamy reality of its purported subject. When Freud describes the creative writer as a 'strange being' about whom we are 'intensely curious' (131), he is in part describing himself. He begins with a sort of theatrical exasperation, as he exclaims: 'If we could at least discover in ourselves or in people like ourselves an activity which was in some way akin to creative writing!' (Freud 1985, 131). A vague air of hopelessness, however, rapidly gives way to a characteristically bold flourish of rhetorical questions: 'Should we not look for the first traces of imaginative activity as early as in childhood? The child's best-loved and most intense occupation is with his [or her] play or games. Might we not say that every child at play behaves like a creative writer . . .?' (131). This prompts a crucial insight: every creative writing class is full of phantom children (and phantom parents). As Adam Phillips comments, 'Freud encourages us to read as we dream, according to our desire, surprised by what may strike us, and unable to predict what will haunt us' (Phillips 2006, xv). Reading Freud is one of the best ways in which to enrich one's sense of what a creative writer is – polymorphously perverse, scarcely articulate, surrounded by 'imagined objects and situations' (132).

Teaching

As will perhaps be evident from the preceding paragraphs, these three 'impossible professions' are intimately linked to one another. Just as psychoanalysis began with the impossible but manifestly productive scenario of Freud analysing himself, and just as his strange science came to be known as 'the talking cure', so creative writing might be conceived as a peculiar sort of auto-analysis. It is also a form of self-teaching that has to do with what is 'other' to the self. The philosopher Maurice Merleau-Ponty's remark seems especially apposite in this context: 'My own words take me by surprise and teach me what to think' (Merleau-Ponty 1964, 88; our translation). It is not simply a matter of becoming a sort of empty screen and watching and learning from the writing that wafts up in front of you, as if it has been written by someone else or by some magical agency. But there is a bit of that, for this is one of the disarming things about creative writing: it is never entirely personal, fully calculated and completely foreseen. It also calls for critical thinking. The writer is always dicing with the unforeseeable. You have to be ready.

Get ready now.

Further reading

For further discussion of topics in this chapter, see 'Creative Writing' in Bennett and Royle (2023). For a complex and richly informative account of 'the rise of creative writing', especially in the context of modern American fiction, see Mark McGurl's *The Program Era: Postwar Fiction and the Rise of Creative Writing* (2009), and for a thought-provoking account of how Amazon has transformed the creative writing industry, see McGurl's more recent *Everything and Less* (2021). In their *Creative Criticism: An Anthology and Guide* (2014) Stephen Benson and Clare Connors provide a good selection of work that explores, questions and unsettles the distinctions between creative and critical writing. For an excellent collection of Freud's work in relation to creative writing, see his *Writings on Art and Literature* (1997). Patrick J. Mahony's *Freud as a Writer* (1987) offers a fine overview of the rhetorical crafting of Freud's own texts, while Mark Edmundson's *Towards Reading Freud: Self-Creation in Milton, Wordsworth, Emerson and Sigmund Freud* (1990) and Perry Meisel's *The Literary Freud* (2007) explore the rich terrain of the literary *in* Freud. Jeremy Tambling's *Literature and Psychoanalysis* (2012) is a lucid and very readable introduction to its Janus-headed subject. On creative writing and dreaming, see Nicholas Royle's *Hélène Cixous: Dreamer, Realist, Analyst, Writing* (2020).

11. Writing short fiction

Not everyone studying literature wants to do creative writing, and short fiction is only one kind among others. Even if you plan never to write short stories or produce any other sort of creative writing as long as you live, this chapter may nevertheless be of some interest. In particular, we hope that it might stimulate and provoke further thinking about the nature of fiction, its purposes and possibilities.

Every writer has a different way of doing what they do. What Bennett and Royle have to say about how to write a work of short fiction may be quite different from what others might say. Take us, if you like, with a pinch of salt. What follows is simply an A–Z of suggestions for writing short fiction.

a. Think in advance about what kind of writing might be worth the effort. If it isn't going to be about the world, if it isn't based on some sort of critically thoughtful response to something real (a dead mouse you found in the cupboard, the enormity of the geopolitics of North Korea, Ukraine, Syria or Palestine, an accident in Peru, a waterfall in New Zealand), it isn't worth doing. The world doesn't need fiction that merely passes the time. There is too much to respond to, to be responsible to, and even responsible for. Fiction has to respond, and you need to be clear what you are trying to respond to.

b. Manuals of creative writing tend to harp on about 'writing from your own experience', but this often opens up a can of worms. Hardly anyone – your mother or father or lover, if you're lucky – is really interested in Your Own Experience. What is 'your own experience'

DOI: 10.4324/9781003301363-14

anyway? Does it refer only to what you've actually seen, witnessed, participated in, firsthand? Does that include what you've read? And the actual experience of writing? Or is it supposed to exclude those? Your own experience is indelibly marked, affected, inflected by language. What happens to you may be singular and unprecedented but needs to be framed with a certain critical detachment – think Dickens, Woolf, Baldwin, Ellison, Rhys or Claudia Rankine.

c. What is important is often what is difficult or painful. Even, for example, writing devoted to the dispassionate observation of an untroubled individual or a peaceful landscape bears testament to what is real, to mortality and transience. The best writing tends to draw on something traumatic, whether it is the experience of happiness (joy can be traumatic) or physical injury or psychological loss. It might be productive to consider writing about something that is in some sense *impossible* for you to write about just *because it is traumatic*. The word 'traumatic' comes from the ancient Greek 'trauma', meaning 'wound'. Creative writing originates in something wounding. In his marvellous book about photography, *Camera Lucida* (1982), Roland Barthes argues that a powerful image always contains some sort of *punctum* – a small detail that punches, punctures, moves the viewer in an unexpected and enigmatic way. Think about the possibilities of an equivalent of the *punctum* in the context of short fiction.

d. What spurs your writing need not be named as such. You might write *about* it by writing *around* the trauma, making the trauma a sort of hidden or oblique presence. You do not need to spell out the wound or point at it and say *Look, here is the trauma*. In the end the wound matters not only because it is yours but in the ways that it is *not* yours: its power and interest lie in how it can be shared (with your reader), relinquished to language (the world of fiction).

e. Humour is something else. Not everyone expresses it in equal measure or has the same sense of it. And like language itself, humour is not something that anyone can own. It is a gift, as well as a riddle. As Freud makes clear in his essay 'Humour' (1927), it is strangely 'liberating and elevating' (Freud 1985, 432). At the same time, it can be anarchic and subversive. As Freud puts it: 'Humour is not resigned; it is rebellious' (429). Moreover, it is never simply opposed to what is serious. As Freud's essay also suggests, the classic and most essential kind, after all, is so-called 'gallows humour'. His example is of the criminal being led out to the gallows on a Monday morning and remarking, 'Well, the week's beginning nicely.'

f. Death is the only real authority for a piece of creative writing. This is Walter Benjamin's point in his great essay 'The Storyteller'. He writes: 'Death is the sanction of everything that the storyteller can tell. He has borrowed his authority from death' (Benjamin 1969, 94). All narratives are ultimately impelled by a sense of mortality, fragility and transience. Nothing lasts. The greatest works of short fiction – Anton Chekhov's, for example, or Katherine Mansfield's – show this most clearly. They are works of gentleness, sometimes shockingly so, but, like their tubercular authors, they are never far from death.

g. It is often said that you should show, not tell. This is not bad advice, as writing comes alive when an idea or a place or a scene or a person is not just described but put into play, set in action. You don't have to explain everything. Don't dillydally with your scene-setting: don't, whatever you do, try to be Henry James. Don't get stuck in an overly long description of what is going on in a character's mind or body. It is best to keep things moving along – without, however, being unduly (tiresomely) snappy.

h. Remember Ernest Hemingway's 'iceberg theory' (seven-eighths of the story should be hidden), or what Bennett and Royle are tempted to call the 'holey' text. Say more by saying less. Let the text breathe: in order to breathe, a work of fiction needs holes, unspoken gaps, missing edges.

i. The traumatic always goes beyond speech, beyond writing, even if it is something seemingly tiny or banal (the cruelty of something a sibling says or does, a bunch of flowers smashed by the rain). That's one of the ways in which creative writing, writing a piece of fiction, engages with the impossible.

j. The impossible in creative writing: this might be a good place to pop in a word about deconstruction. 'The least bad definition of deconstruction', according to Jacques Derrida, is: 'the *experience of the impossible*' (Derrida 1992b, 200). Deconstruction, then, has a special place when it comes to thinking about literature (or creative writing). Literature is slippery, ghostly, without essence. To think deconstructively is to think about how literary works open up, or open us up, to experiencing the impossible.

k. You should write on your nerve, as D.H. Lawrence would say, write as often and as much as you can. Once you have started, keep going. (But for health-and-safety reasons, we hesitate to recommend taking too closely after Franz Kafka, who would remain at his desk writing all day, all night, until the story was done.)

l. It can be like dreaming – if you move on waking, you'll start to forget it. When you write, once you are under way, it can be worth staying under way, keep it flowing, keep it going, until you have a first draft. The thought of writing here might be compared to Keats' image of Adam's dream: 'he awoke and found it truth' (Keats 2005, 54).

m. Once you have a first draft, you are in paradise. It is a fool's paradise, of course, but take a break, enjoy the exhilaration of having got this far. You have only just begun.

n. For then comes the second draft, and the second draft is very often more a matter of cutting than of adding. See how much you can take away or take out. Think, once again, of Hemingway. His 'iceberg theory' emerged out of writing a story called 'Out of Season' in 1923. In a later memoir, *A Moveable Feast*, he recalled that he had cut out the 'real end' of the story, in which the old man hangs himself: 'This was omitted on my new theory that you could omit anything', Hemingway commented, 'and the omitted part would strengthen the story and make people feel something more than they understood' (Hemingway 2011, 71).

o. If you say something or have a character say something in ten words rather than twenty, or in five rather than ten, you are making progress. What goes for critical writing goes for creative writing: if in doubt, cut it out. Once you have a second draft, read it aloud, preferably to another human (but a hamster may also suffice). Reading your piece of writing aloud is a crucial ploy for catching unnecessary words or phrases, dull patches, sloppy punctuation, unnecessary slowings in pace, too much information. A piece of short fiction should *sound* good.

p. Dialogue is especially challenging in writing fiction. It is good to have it: it offers more voices, other voices. Bear in mind Elizabeth Bowen's insight that 'speech is what characters *do to each other*' (Bowen 1962, 253). Dialogue needs to *do* as well as say. And you need to show how characters are affecting each other by the things they are saying. Everything a character says should do something. This might take the form of: (1) a performative utterance (saying something that is some kind of promise, or threat, or challenge, or confession, or naming, or revealing, or concealing); (2) moving the narrative on and *enriching the dynamic of character relations*; (3) deepening our knowledge and appreciation of the character or interlocutor (an instance of pretence, betrayal, evasion, something notably painful or humorous or ironic and so on).

q. Critics often talk about epiphanies in short stories (as we have done in 'Reading a Short Story'). In other words, a passage, sentence, clause or even a single word can function as a moment of revelation for the text as a whole. You do not need to have selected and crafted an epiphany for your text, but a careful reader is likely to be alert to it in any case, even if only unconsciously. 'Epiphany' is not the only term for this. An alternative name might be the black box of the text, the point where everything is gathered together, analysis of which yields a crucial understanding of the structure, flight and fate of the writing. At some point in the writing process (perhaps not until it is all over), you might find it helpful to ask yourself: is there a black box and, if so, where is it? It may take you, not to mention your reader, some time to find the box. Sometimes, for example, in the short fiction of Kafka or Beckett, you discover it is in fact less a question of a box than of something like a black hole, something that emits no light and sucks all into its abyssal darkness.

r. And then there is the turn, or turning-point, for which one name would be Aristotle's *peripeteia* ('reversal', 'sudden change of fortune'). Elizabeth Bowen claims that 'a story, to be a story, *must* have a turning-point' (Bowen 1986, 122). The story is going along in one way, and perhaps everything seems tickety-boo, routine, flowing along, but then there is a turn: something untoward happens. There is a change of perspective (narrative or temporal), things transpire to be other than they seemed and so on. A story without a turning-point is like a story without hope. But don't make it into a complete mad-house. When people start out writing short fiction they often imagine it is ok to have all sorts of characters, shifts in time, strings of events and so on. That is, almost always, an error.

s. As with everything else involving a specific craft or skill — being a carpenter, a lawyer or a teacher — you may expect to need thousands of hours of 'work experience' before you really know your way around. But here is a tip for one short cut: don't try to cram too much in. You're not writing *The Odyssey*. There are reasons it is a work of short fiction, not a novella or a novel. The whole beauty (and, as we might say, the hole beauty) of the thing is, as Edgar Allan Poe recognized, that you can read the piece 'at one sitting', and that it all comes down to the production of 'a certain unique or single *effect*' (Poe 1965, 106–108). Think small. Have as few characters as is necessary for the narrative (but be wary of having only one, above all on account of the risks of self-indulgence, self-centredness and a sort of suffocating monopoly).

t. The title: at some point in the proceedings you are going to have to attend to this. It may come to you only at the end, or you might have the title before you start. A good title is a ticket to pleasure, a kind of promise of what is to come. Of course you can plump for a downbeat, prosaic sort of title, as V.S. Pritchett tends to do: 'The Sailor', 'Citizen', 'The Speech'. Or you can veer in the opposite direction, towards the explicitly strange or dramatic, as in Poe: 'The Fall of the House of Usher', 'The Imp of the Perverse', 'The Balloon Hoax'. But there is no harm in aiming for something in between, a title that has a faint sense of intrigue or oddness, of danger or allure. Eudora Welty's stories, for instance, include 'The Worn Path', 'At the Landing' and 'The Whole World Knows' – titles that might easily prompt you to wonder 'what path and why worn?', 'what landing and what happens there?' and 'the whole world knows *what*?' A good title might be short, such as Raymond Carver's provocative 'Fat', or it might be long, as in his poignant 'What We Talk About When We Talk About Love', but it is always worth trying to come up with a title that tickles you, a word or phrase that may in turn intrigue and delight your reader.

u. Sometimes a title can actually function as a piece of wisdom for writing short stories, as in Grace Paley's witty and provoking 'Enormous Changes at the Last Minute'. Remember the enormous change that Hemingway made by omitting the suicide of the old man in 'Out of Season'. You shouldn't necessarily expect to make enormous changes at the last minute, but it can happen that, when you are reading over your piece in what you hope is its final draft, you see something you could alter that might seem small but would make a great difference to the quality of your work. It might be a matter of cutting something out, or changing something a character says, or adding some telling final detail. Enormous change is, of course, relative. What strikes you at the time as enormous might seem tiny to someone else. (It is like the character in Poe's story, 'The Sphinx', who, with a sense of horror, watches a monster making its way from the horizon down the hillside towards the house, until he realizes it is an insect on the windowpane.)

v.   In the end, however, you should feel that your piece is as good as you can make it. You need to be able to let go. Shakespeare could let go. There comes a point when you have to say goodbye. The point at which to let go is when you have all your ducks in a line, every word is doing the work you want it to do, every item of punctuation is right. Raymond Carver memorably describes knowing when you have finished with a story, in his brief essay 'On Writing': 'Evan Connell said once that he knew he was finished with a short story when he found himself going through it and taking out commas and then going through the story again and putting commas back in the same places' (Carver 1986, 24).

w.   Bear in mind what Frank Kermode called 'the sense of an ending' (1966) or the importance of what Peter Brooks so richly explores under the heading, 'reading for the plot' (1984). However captivated your reader might be – by your subject-matter; your voice or style; your characters and dialogue; your descriptions of places, events, feelings; or the intellectual or philosophical richness of your writing – you also need to tell a story. And a story has to have an ending. Your readers will be looking for a narrative, and a narrative cannot not end. Indeed, readers will seek to impose narrative coherence on your work even if you do not. (Robert Coover's 'The Baby-Sitter' (1969) is a classic example of a story that seeks, with doubtless only limited success, to subvert or destroy these readerly presuppositions and desires.) Readers, of course, do not necessarily – and indeed often do not at all – just want a rudimentary linear narrative. Readers can take pleasure in being held up, sent off in odd directions, they can enjoy a feeling of veering, a sudden change or turn, an undoing of expectations – *so long as* you will have told a story in the end. Readers always read with 'the sense of an ending'.

x.   But don't strain yourself with the need to end with a bang. Rather than fret about having an ending that is sufficiently 'dramatic', 'revelatory', 'final' and so on, you might think about ending in a more low-key, unexpected way. Some of the most powerful endings to short stories are endings that do not really end – so-called 'open endings', or endings that turn away from the principal action and concerns of the story and invite the reader (perhaps in an annoying or disquieting way) to focus on something else. Kafka's great story 'A Hunger Artist', for example, closes not with the emaciated figure with whom we have been concerned from the beginning, now finally starved to death and lying in the straw of his cage, but with an image of the 'leaping', 'noble body' (Kafka 1992, 277) of a panther, the creature that has replaced him and that now compels everyone's attention.

y. It is notable that Kafka should have ended his work with the image of a non-human animal. The rapport between the literary work and animals is perhaps strongest in poetry, but it is not an entirely stupid idea to consider the short story, also, especially liable to figure – and figure *as* – some sort of animal. The short story would be a strange creature. It might seem to come from nowhere, and soon enough it will disappear again. It should have an unexpected, otherworldly quality, like the moose in Elizabeth Bishop. 'The Moose' (Bishop 1991, 169–173) is not a short story but a narrative poem. It is about a bus full of people travelling inland from the sea, at night in the fog, until the driver 'stops with a jolt' because a moose has emerged from 'the impenetrable wood' and has halted before them.

> Taking her time,
> she looks the bus over,
> grand, otherworldly.

The creature produces a 'sweet / sensation of joy' in all who look at her. Then the bus moves on.

z. Poems can also tell stories, then, and provide a last thought here. 'In poetry,' writes Wallace Stevens, 'you must love the words, the ideas and images and rhythms with all your capacity to love anything at all' (Stevens 1997, 902). The same goes for writing a short story. If it is worth doing at all, writing fiction demands your body and soul, heart and mind. You should love and care for every word, every sentence of the strange object you have made. You cannot be sure what your reader might think or feel, or even if your work will ever be read, but that love and care for what you have written is perhaps finally what most matters.

Further reading

The best further reading for writing short fiction is undoubtedly short fiction itself – as produced, for example, by any or all of the following: Heinrich von Kleist, Edgar Allan Poe, E.T.A. Hoffmann, Herman Melville, Nathaniel Hawthorne, Guy de Maupassant, Nikolai Gogol, Anton Chekhov, Henry James, Joseph Conrad, Virginia Woolf, Franz

Kafka, James Joyce, D.H. Lawrence, Katherine Mansfield, Zora Neale Hurston, Ernest Hemingway, Elizabeth Bowen, Jorge Luis Borges, Flannery O'Connor, Clarice Lispector, J.G. Ballard, Angela Carter, Raymond Carver, David Foster Wallace, Lydia Davis, Jayne Anne Phillips, Richard Ford, Jackie Kay, Alice Munro and Vanessa Onwuemezi. Among the most stimulating critical essays by such writers, see Carver's brief but brilliant 'On Writing'. Although focused on the longer form of the novel, Bowen's 'Notes on Writing a Novel' (in Bowen 1986) is also full of fascinating perceptions and insights. Walter Benjamin's 'The Storyteller' is a profound meditation on the art of fiction, long and short. For further reading on notions of trauma, see the chapters on 'Loss' and 'Wounds' in Bennett and Royle (2023).

Appendix: The wordbook

'Wordbook' might be a good name for a novel or a play or a collection of poems or a piece of creative non-fiction. As it happens, however, it is another name for a dictionary, a lexicon. The three words 'dictionary', 'lexicon', 'wordbook' are interchangeable, but each has a slightly different resonance. Whatever you call it, the word-book is an essential tool for studying literature. You are spoilt for choice in this area, with a number of excellent dictionaries in print or online, including *The Chambers Dictionary*, the *Oxford Dictionary of English*, *Collins English Dictionary*, *Merriam-Webster's American English Dictionary* or Google's *English Dictionary* function. Then there is the behemoth, the *Oxford English Dictionary*, usually known as the '*OED*' and first completed in 1928 – of which more in a moment.

Consulting a good dictionary can be one of the chief delights of reading and writing: it enables you to take a pause without losing the plot. It is also a way of slowly but surely expanding your mind. As far as a single-volume dictionary is concerned, the go-to option for Bennett and Royle is *Chambers*. *The Chambers Dictionary* is particularly rich in the range of its literary references. It is also at times surprisingly witty. Here are just a couple of definitions: to 'bugger off' is decorously construed as to 'go away quickly', and a 'leaf' is initially defined in rather ponderously scientific terms as 'one of the lateral organs developed from the stem or axis of a plant below its growing-point' but then (as if the editor at *Chambers* is giving up and just pointing): 'one of those flat green structures'.

All good dictionaries offer a wealth of information. Although most people turn to a dictionary to check the meaning or the spelling of a word, all the information is potentially useful. Dictionaries usually explain:

- How the word is spelled, including any variations in spelling
- Its pronunciation: for example, prō-nun-si-ā'shən in *Chambers*, or the more technical transcription of the word in the *OED* as /prəʃnʌnsɪˈeɪʃn/
- The grammatical name for the word in question (noun ('n.'), adjective ('adj.'), adverb ('adv.'), etc.)
- What the word means
- Its etymology – where or how the word in question originates.

To return to the behemoth, the *OED* is massive – twenty large volumes in the print version of the 1989 second edition, but now, in electronic form, even larger. Any good library should have a print copy or offer access to the online version. The reason the *OED* is so much bigger than your average wordbook is not just because it defines more words but because it is a historical dictionary. This means that, in addition to the current senses of words, it offers information about when the words entered the language and how their usage has changed over time. And it gives examples of usage so you can see the word in action for yourself.

The way that words change over time is particularly important for a historical discipline such as literary studies. And for this reason the *OED* is a crucial resource. The senses of words alter and shift over time, acquiring and losing nuances; words evolve new and separate meanings, they drop out of the language and become 'obsolete'. It is easy to be misled by the modern sense of a word when it is used in an older text and easy to overlook the multiple senses of a word that a text might be exploiting.

In his famous 'To be or not to be' speech, for example, Hamlet uses the word 'conscience': 'Thus conscience does make cowards of us all' he says (*Hamlet*, 3.1.84). He is outlining why people don't usually do away with themselves – it is the 'dread' of the unknown that stops us committing suicide, he concludes, and that makes us 'bear those ills we have' rather than 'fly[ing] to others that we know not of' (ll. 82–83). Most critics agree that Hamlet is here referring not only to the modern sense of the 'conscience' as a personal ethical code that guides one's actions but to a separate sense of the word, one that lacks this ethical dimension and that has largely fallen into disuse: Hamlet's 'conscience' is, in effect, 'consciousness', one's 'internal conviction, personal awareness', as the *OED* puts it (*OED*, 'conscience', n.7a). It is ambiguous: it is not just about ethics but also a question of awareness: not knowing what happens after death means that we fear it. Similarly, in reading *Hamlet*, it would be easy to be baffled by the modern English sense of 'quoted' as meaning to 'reproduce or repeat a passage from a book' (*OED*, 'quoted', v, I.2.a) when Polonius says that he regrets that he has not better 'quoted' Hamlet (2.1.109). What he means, however, is that he wishes he had better 'noticed', 'observed' or 'scrutinized' the anguished prince (*OED*, 'quote', v, II.5.a). These distinctions matter. It is in such differences, in these nuances or implications or connotations of words, that literary texts most richly and profoundly cast their verbal spell.

Glossary

Alienation effect: concept and strategy originally introduced by the German playwright and poet Bertolt Brecht (1898–1956). A piece of theatre should not reassure or console the spectator with easy, recognizable characters and psychology. The dramatic work should on the contrary seek to disturb and alter the audience's (bourgeois or other unreflective or indoctrinated) assumptions and beliefs through a deliberate effect or effects of alienating the audience.

Alliteration: repeated consonant sounds, particularly at the beginning of words, for example, 'kiddies' clobber', 'mountains of moonstone'. (See also **assonance**.)

Allusion: a reference, often only implicit or indirect, to another work of literature or art, person, event and so on; sometimes referred to as 'echo'. (See also **intertextuality**.)

Analepsis: the literary critical term for 'flashback' in film: the rhetorical figure that describes a shift in temporal perspective in a narrative back to something that happened earlier in the story.

Anaphora: the rhetorical figure for the repetition of a word or phrase at the beginning of successive sentences, clauses or lines of verse.

Aphorism: a concise sentence or statement purporting to formulate a truth, phrased in a thought-provoking, arresting and sometimes witty manner. An aphorism is similar to a proverb but is distinguished by the fact that it is not anonymous. Celebrated authors of aphorisms include Blaise Pascal, William Blake, Oscar Wilde and Sarah Manguso.

Aporia: from the ancient Greek word for something that is impassable (literally a blockage in a road or passage), aporia is a rhetorical figure for doubt. Especially associated with deconstructive thinking, an aporia may arise

when the reader encounters two or more incompatible codes, meanings or
'messages'.

Aposiopesis: from the Greek 'becoming silent', aposiopesis is the rhetorical term
for a sentence or statement that breaks off in mid-stream, an unfinished . . .
(An ellipsis or three dots are often used to represent such moments.)

Assonance: correspondence or 'rhyming' of vowel sounds, for example eat,
sleep; ooze, droop.

Autofiction: a term coined by the French writer Serge Doubrovsky in 1977, it
refers to a fictionalized version of a person's life: an autofiction is an autobio-
graphical novel but one that – like D.H. Lawrence's *Sons and Lovers* (1913),
James Joyce's *A Portrait of the Artist as a Young Man* (1916) and Sylvia Plath's
The Bell Jar (1963), or more recently works by W.G. Sebald, Rachel Cusk and
Yiyun Li – deliberately departs from historical or biographical circumstance.

Bibliophagy, bibliophagous: book-devouring. Literal in the case of rats and
worms, figurative in the case of those who love to read books.

Close reading: a method or practice of reading particularly associated with the
so-called New Critics of the mid-twentieth century that emphasizes careful
attention to 'the words on the page' rather than to historical and ideological
contexts, the biography or intentions of the author, readers' responses and so
on. In fact, however, close reading may be considered the fundamental skill or
technique that is developed in the academic study of literature, and in recent
decades it has been combined with or integrated into approaches that focus
on more general thematic, political, cultural and ideological considerations in
the interpretation of literary texts.

Context: literally, that which accompanies or surrounds a text. To quote (a line
from Stevie Smith, for instance) is always to take that line out of its context.
A careful critical reading invariably seeks to take account of the text in which
the quoted line, phrase, sentence or passage occurs. More generally, 'context'
refers to the setting or framing, which might therefore entail the historical
context, the geographical or environmental context, the cultural or political
context and so on, in which a text is written or read. It is easy enough to see
that 'context' is a bottomless can of worms. As Jacques Derrida consistently
argues, nothing can be determined out of context, but no context can be
limited or exhaustively accounted for.

Creative reading: in the sense particularly developed by Bennett and Royle,
creative reading is a mode of reading that seeks to be careful, faithful and
accurate in its response to the text and its contexts and, at the same time,
to lead on to new, even unthought-of perspectives, emphases and concerns.

Criticism: in this context, 'criticism' refers to the formal analysis, interpretation and evaluation of literary texts. 'Criticism' in this sense should not be

confused simply with 'fault-finding' or the 'passing of *unfavourable* judgments' (*OED*), both of which are, if present at all, distinctly minor aspects of the work of the literary critic.

Death drive: concept elaborated upon by Sigmund Freud, initially in *Beyond the Pleasure Principle* (1920). Freud argues that there are two principles that may be conventionally understood to govern life: the 'pleasure principle', which involves the desire to eat, drink, touch, have sex, possess or otherwise have what you want, and the 'reality principle', which regulates and keeps the pleasure principle in check (no, you must not shoot the president, have sex with a ferret, etc.). Besides or beyond these principles, however, Freud speculates on the furtive and **uncanny** existence of something darker – the workings of the death drive or 'Thanatos', a (mostly silent or unconscious) self-destructiveness in the individual. In his later work Freud opens the concept up in other ways too, inviting us to consider it an energy or impulse that (however inadvertently or surreptitiously) drives the behaviour of nation-states and even humanity in general. He also comes to associate the death drive, in various ways, with sadism and the desire for mastery. (Sometimes 'death instinct'; also plural, 'death instincts'.)

Deconstruction: a word made famous by Jacques Derrida (1930–2004), sometimes still used in the sense it acquired in the 1980s, namely as a philosophical and political approach to thinking about culture, history, literature and everything else you might care to think of. In particular, it was associated with looking at texts with an eye or ear for incongruities, contradictions and aporias, or for the importance of the seemingly marginal, excluded or unsaid. Nowadays the word 'deconstruction' is often used quite loosely as a synonym for 'dismantling', 'demystifying', 'exposing the hidden prejudices or contradictions of' or even just criticizing something – a text, a system, a person and so on. In its more radical form, 'deconstruction' retains a crucial link with other motifs explored by Derrida such as the undecidable and the experience of the impossible. (See also **undecidable** and **impossible**.)

Double bind a double bind involves the kind of double or contradictory statement or order which deconstructive criticism tends to focus on. For example, the sentence 'This sentence is not true' is both true and not true at the same time (if it's true then it's not true and if it's not true then it's true). Rather differently, the sentence 'Do not read this sentence' involves an order which can only be obeyed if it is disobeyed (we have to read the sentence in order to know that we should not read it).

Ekphrasis, ekphrastic: from the Greek for 'description', ekphrasis denotes the attempt by a work in one medium to represent a work in another; often used to refer to a poem that describes a picture or other artwork such as John

Keats's 'Ode on a Grecian Urn', W.H. Auden's 'Musée des Beaux Arts' or John Ashbery's *Self Portrait in a Convex Mirror*.

Elegy: (Gk. 'lament') a poem of mourning for an individual or a lament for a tragic event; the adjective 'elegiac' may be used to describe a sense of mourning or loss encountered in any text – poem or prose.

Enjambment: the phenomenon whereby one line of poetry carries over into the next line without a syntactical pause or punctuation.

Epiphany: a moment of special illumination or sudden revelation. Originally a religious term referring to the manifestation of Christ to the Wise Men, it was adapted by James Joyce in more secular mode in his early novel *Stephen Hero* (1904–6).

Epistolary: adjective, to do with letters and letter-writing; novels written entirely in the form of letters are called 'epistolary novels', a particularly common form in eighteenth-century literature.

Essentialism: refers to ways of conceiving people, cultures and so on as having certain innate, natural or universal characteristics. Essentialism is strongly contested in much contemporary literary theory. The following three statements are all examples of essentialist thinking: (1) 'I have a personality, an individuality, which is completely unaffected by anything out there in the "real" world, such as language, economics, education, nationality and so on'; (2) 'Women are more intelligent, caring and sensitive than men'; and (3) Black people excel at sport.

Focalization: term used to refer to the way in which a narrative is told from the perspective or point of view of one or more characters: events are 'seen' or imagined through the mind of certain individuals.

Free indirect speech (or free indirect discourse): refers to narrative written in the third person (from an apparently external point of view, describing what 'he', 'she', 'they' do) but carrying with it knowledge or apparent knowledge of what 'he', 'she', 'they' are thinking, feeling or perceiving. The narrative moves unmarked from the perspective of the third-person narrator into the minds or perspective of the character. Closely related to notions of **magical thinking**, **omniscient narrator** and **telepathy**.

Hermeneutic: a term formerly used to designate attempts to establish a set of rules governing the interpretation of the Bible in the nineteenth century; in the context of contemporary criticism, the term refers to acts or theories of interpretation more generally.

Impossible: in some contexts associated with what is futile or pointless, the word 'impossible' can also be a trigger for action, transformation or revolution. When Freud says that there are three 'impossible professions' (government, psychoanalysis and teaching), he does not mean we should consider them all useless and just give up. In its most radical form the affirmative or transformative sense of the impossible comes in Jacques Derrida's notion of deconstruction as 'a certain experience of the impossible'. Even or especially if something is impossible (justice, for example, or unconditional hospitality or forgiveness), this does not mean we cannot or should not desire it, dream of it, try to make it happen.

Intertextuality: a term coined by Julia Kristeva to refer to the fact that texts are constituted by what Roland Barthes calls a 'tissue of citations', that every word of every text refers to other texts and so on, limitlessly. Often used in an imprecise or weak sense to talk about echoes or allusions.

Irony: a rhetorical figure referring to the sense that there is a discrepancy between words and their meanings, between actions and their results, or between appearance and reality: most simply, saying one thing and meaning another.

Lacuna (plural, lacunae): a hiatus in the text, a moment where something appears to be missing.

Literary theory: 'the field of study concerned with inquiry into the evaluation, analysis, and understanding of literary works and (now also) other texts . . . often incorporating concepts from other disciplines, such as philosophy, politics, or sociology' (*OED*). Literary theory is often associated with certain important schools of thought from the second half of the twentieth and the early twenty-first centuries, including formalism, structuralism, deconstruction, poststructuralism, new historicism, feminism, queer theory, postcolonialism, trauma theory, ecocriticism and so on.

Magical thinking: a term used by psychiatrists and psychologists to refer to the delusions, firmly held superstitious or paranoid beliefs that an individual might maintain. Such a person hears imaginary voices, believes that his / her own thoughts can be overheard, is convinced that in order to be safe s/he must perform certain actions over and over again and so on. While such beliefs can be an element in frightening and debilitating psychiatric conditions, in milder forms magical thinking is extremely common in everyday life and is indeed the very oxygen of literature. There is no novel or short story that does not depend on telling the reader what a character is thinking or feeling and on other forms of magical thinking.

Meta–: (from the Greek 'meta', meaning 'with', 'beside') this prefix has proved helpful in a range of critical terms. The following instances are especially common: **metalinguistic** refers to language about language; **metatheatrical** (also, **metadramatic**) refers to the way in which a play or some aspect of a play (a speech, for example, or simply an image) explicitly alerts the reader or audience to the fact that s/he is reading or watching a play; **metafiction**

refers to a work of fiction that explicitly highlights its own status as a story; **metapoetic** refers to the way in which a poem refers to its own status as a poem and so on. (See also **self-reflexivity**.)

Mimesis: (Gk. 'imitation') the idea that literature attempts to represent 'life' or 'the world' more or less accurately, as it 'actually' is. (See also **realism**.)

Mind-reading: a term that can be used to describe what a narrator or narrative does, especially when the text makes the reader a party to what different characters are thinking and feeling, to their pasts or futures and so on. The term also, however, applies to the way that literary texts affect readers: readers are in turn drawn into games of mind-reading (trying to calculate or surmise what motivates a particular character's actions or desires, or to understand the meaning, causes and consequences of a particular event or experience and so on).

Narrator: the person or persona (as distinguished from the author) who is telling a story. Narrators can be variously categorized: a so-called omniscient narrator appears to know everything, an intrusive narrator gives his or her own comments and opinions on the story, an unreliable narrator cannot be trusted for some reason (e.g. he or she is prejudiced, exaggerating, lying), a first-person narrator presents himself or herself in the story as 'I', a third-person narrator speaks of his or her characters as 'she', 'he' and so on.

Omniscient narrator: term used where a narrative is related by an apparently God-like being, an all-knowing narrator who is able to divulge any detail of a character's inner thoughts and feelings, who knows everything that has happened and is going to happen and so on. 'Omniscient' was originally a word reserved for the Judaeo-Christian deity. Any narration (even Biblical narrative) is necessarily partial, restricted, framed and thus limited. Omniscience is a critical fiction that tends to promote or protect a religiously inflected approach to literary works. Bennett and Royle prefer to talk in terms of **telepathic narration**, **mind-reading** and **magical thinking**.

Paraphrase: noun and verb referring to the attempt (often helpful, sometimes unavoidable but never entirely satisfactory or sufficient) to put something in other words, to use 'your own words' to sum up what a given phrase, sentence, passage or text is saying.

Paratext: term referring to any kind of text that is next to or beside (Gk. *para*) the main text. Examples of paratext would include the title of a work, a preface or foreword, the acknowledgements and any so-called end-matter such as an appendix ('The Wordbook', for instance) or this glossary. The notion of paratext always raises questions of borders and framing: is the present glossary, for example, a part of or apart from the main text that precedes it?

Performative: pertaining generally to performance and, in the context of drama, to the active, dynamic effects of theatre. In the context of speech-act theory and the analysis of literary texts, however, 'performative' is an adjective referring to the capacity that statements have for *doing* as well as *saying* things. A promise or an act of naming, for example, is a performative. A poem or novel not only means but *does* something: it moves you, for example, or brings something new into the world.

Philology: literally, the love of words (Gk. *philein* to love, *logos* word); more formally the science of language, especially concerned with its historical development.

Primary text: the literary text that is being discussed, rather than the critical text or texts (including your own essay) that discuss that text.

Prolepsis: the rhetorical term to describe the way that a narrative or other text (including a critical essay) looks ahead, anticipates, tells you something or tells you about something that is going to happen later. Prolepsis is a rough equivalent of what film-goers call the 'flashforward'.

Prosody: the study and analysis of versification, focusing in particular on questions of metre, rhythm, rhyme and other elements of the sound-patterning of a poem.

Realism: a descriptive term, particularly associated with the nineteenth-century novel, to refer to the idea that texts appear to represent 'the world' 'as it really is'. For Bennett and Royle it is more precisely about the way that novels provoke thinking by letting us see how such representations of 'the world' 'as it really is' are fabrications in language. Far from offering us the innocent transparency of a 'window on the world', a realist novel or short story invariably has things to tell us about the power of fiction to make worlds and about the strange, sometimes uncanny borders or distinctions between the real and the fictive. (See also **referential**.)

Referential, referentiality: language is said to be functioning in a referential way when it refers in an apparently unequivocal way to its objects. An international newspaper headline might run: 'Huge explosion in central Cairo.' The reader may wonder what kind of explosion and what 'huge' entails and whereabouts exactly in Cairo, but the way in which such journalistic language functions is held to be referential. The reader makes referential assumptions: the newspaper is referring to some actual explosion (a bomb or such like), not to an 'explosion of interest'; 'Cairo' is the capital of Egypt, not an imaginary place or, say, a small town somewhere in the United States. Certain writers work very hard to maintain a sense of referential language, to avoid ambiguities, metaphors, exaggerations and so on. (See also **realism**.)

Rhetorical trope: a trope (from the ancient Greek word meaning 'turn') is an example of language working in a figurative or non-literal manner. Examples of trope include metaphor, metonymy, hyperbole, litotes and catachresis.

Satire: the humorous presentation of human folly or vice in such a way as to make it look ridiculous, for example Jonathan Swift's *A Modest Proposal* (1729). Conventionally, satire is not merely an attempt to ridicule but to change people's understanding and behaviour. Swift's proposal that small children in Ireland be sold, killed and eaten is powerful satire in part because it articulates a passionate sense of outrage at poverty in Ireland and English attitudes to that poverty at the time in question.

Secondary text, secondary criticism: terms used to refer to texts or writings about another text, in particular critical books, articles or essays about a literary work.

Self-reflexivity: the phenomenon whereby a piece of writing refers to or reflects on itself. Often used interchangeably with 'self-referentiality'. (See also **meta-**.)

Simulacrum: an imitation, image or likeness.

Singularity: term used to refer to something that is unique or special, in some sense without precedent or parallel. To attend to the singularity of F. Scott Fitzgerald's *The Great Gatsby*, for example, would be to try to respond and do justice to what makes this novel different from any and every other novel.

Soliloquy: speech (usually in the context of drama) in which a character can be heard 'thinking aloud'. Hamlet's 'To be or not to be' speech is probably the most often-quoted soliloquy in English literature.

Tautology: term for when something is described or defined in terms of what it is, in other words a repetition of something already evident in the same statement. A celebrated example is Gertrude Stein's 'A rose is a rose is a rose' – along with Virginia Woolf's nicely unsettling reply: 'Is it?'

Telepathy, telepathic narration: useful terms for the description of how literary works are structured, referring to the ways in which the discourse of a novel, for example, is predicated on the idea that we can know what is going on in the minds of different characters. Narration is telepathic in that it tells us what a given character is perceiving, thinking or feeling. It draws the reader into a kind of telepathic world. (See also **mind-reading** and **magical thinking**.)

Uncanny: an adjective made especially rich for literary studies by Freud's essay 'The Uncanny' (1919), 'uncanny' means not simply weird, spooky or strange but entails some disturbance of our sense of what is familiar and unfamiliar. It has to do with a suggestion (but not conviction) of something supernatural going on.

Undecidability, undecidable: the phenomenon or experience of being unable to come to a decision when faced with two or more possible readings or interpretations. In a weak and imprecise sense, used interchangeably with 'indeterminacy'. 'Indeterminacy' is a negative term, however, implying that a decision (about being unable to determine a reading or interpretation) has already been reached. 'Undecidability', on the other hand, stresses the active, continuing challenge to decide.

Verisimilitude: life-likeness; the appearance of being real or true. 'Verisimilitude' is often used in the context of discussions of reality effects, realism and so on.

Bibliography

All quotations from the *OED* are from the *Oxford English Dictionary* online. Unless otherwise stated, quotations from Shakespeare are from Shakespeare, William. 1988. *The Complete Works: Compact Edition*, eds. Stanley Wells and Gary Taylor. Oxford: Clarendon Press. Quotations from the Bible are from the King James version (1611).

Abel, Lionel. 2004. *Tragedy and Metatheatre: Essays on Dramatic Form*. New York: Holmes and Meier.

Adorno, Theodor W. 1991. 'The Essay as Form', in *Notes to Literature*, ed. Rolf Tiedemann, trans. Shierry Weber Nicholsen, vol. 1. New York: Columbia University Press.

Anderson, Linda. 2011. *Autobiography*, 2nd edn. London: Routledge.

Aristotle. 2001. 'Poetics', in *The Norton Anthology of Theory and Criticism*, ed. Vincent B. Leitch. New York: Norton.

Attridge, Derek. 2004. *The Singularity of Literature*. London: Routledge.

Attridge, Derek and Henry Staten. 2015. *The Craft of Poetry: Dialogues on Minimal Interpretation*. London: Routledge.

Atwood, Margaret. 2002. *Negotiating with the Dead: A Writer on Writing*. Cambridge: Cambridge University Press.

Auden, W.H. 1979. *Selected Poems*, ed. Edward Mendelson. London: Faber and Faber.

Augustine, Saint. 1992. *Confessions*, trans. Henry Chadwick. Oxford: Oxford University Press.

Austen, Jane. 2006a. *Pride and Prejudice*, ed. Pat Rogers. Cambridge: Cambridge University Press.

Austen, Jane. 2006b. *Persuasion*, eds. Janet Todd and Antje Blank. Cambridge: Cambridge University Press.

Austin, J.L. 1962. *How to Do Things with Words*. Oxford: Clarendon Press.

Baker, J.A. 2010. *The Peregrine: The Hill of Summer & Diaries. The Complete Works of J. A. Baker*, ed. John Fanshawe. London: Collins.

Baker, J.A. 2017. *The Peregrine*. London: William Collins.

Barkan, Leonard. 2001. 'What Did Shakespeare Read?' in *The Cambridge Companion to Shakespeare*, eds. Margreta de Grazia and Stanley Wells. Cambridge: Cambridge University Press.

Barker, Howard. 2005. *Death, the One and the Art of Theatre*. Abingdon: Routledge.

Barthes, Roland. 1982. *Camera Lucida: Reflections on Photography*, trans. Richard Howard. London: Jonathan Cape.

Barthes, Roland. 1986. 'The Reality Effect', in *The Rustle of Language*, trans. Richard Howard. New York: Hill and Wang.

Barthes, Roland. 1990. *The Pleasure of the Text*, trans. Richard Miller. Oxford: Basil Blackwell.

Bate, Jonathan. 1997. *The Romantics on Shakespeare*. London: Penguin.

Bate, Jonathan. 2010. *English Literature: A Very Short Introduction*. Oxford: Oxford University Press.

Bateson, Gregory. 1973. *Steps to An Ecology of Mind: Collected Essays in Anthropology, Psychiatry, Evolution and Epistemology*. London: Granada.

Beckett, Samuel. 1990. 'Stirrings Still', in *As the Story Was Told: Uncollected and Late Prose*. London: John Calder.

Beckett, Samuel. 2006. *The Complete Dramatic Works*. London: Faber and Faber.

Beckett, Samuel. 2009. *Watt*, ed. C.J. Ackerley. London: Faber and Faber.

Benjamin, Walter. 1969. 'The Storyteller', trans. Harry Zohn, in *Illuminations: Essays and Reflections*, ed. Hannah Arendt. New York: Schocken Books.

Bennett, Andrew and Nicholas Royle. 2023. *An Introduction to Literature, Criticism and Theory*, 6th edn. London: Routledge.

Benson, Stephen and Clare Connors, eds. 2014. *Creative Criticism: An Anthology and Guide*. Edinburgh: Edinburgh University Press.

Bewes, Timothy. 2022. *Free Indirect: The Novel in a Postfictional Age*. New York: Columbia University Press.

Bishop, Elizabeth. 1991. *The Complete Poems 1927–1979*. New York: Noonday Press.

Blanchot, Maurice. 1982. *The Space of Literature*, trans. Ann Smock. Lincoln, NE: University of Nebraska Press.

Bloom, Harold. 1999. *Shakespeare: The Invention of the Human*. London: Fourth Estate.

Bowen, Elizabeth. 1943. *The Hotel*. Harmondsworth: Penguin.

Bowen, Elizabeth. 1950. 'Preface to The Faber Book of Modern Short Stories', in *Collected Impressions*. London: Longmans, Green and Co.

Bowen, Elizabeth. 1962. *Afterthought: Pieces About Writing*. London: Longmans.

Bowen, Elizabeth. 1964. *The Little Girls*. Harmondsworth: Penguin.

Bowen, Elizabeth. 1986. *The Mulberry Tree*. London: Virago.

Boxall, Peter, ed. 2010. 'Thinking Poetry', special issue of *Textual Practice*, 24:4.

Boxall, Peter. 2013. *Twenty-First Century Fiction*. Cambridge: Cambridge University Press.

Boxall, Peter. 2020. *The Prosthetic Imagination: A History of the Novel as Artificial Life*. Cambridge: Cambridge University Press.

Boxall, Peter and Michael Jonik, eds. 2016. '30@30: The Future of Literary Thinking', *Textual Practice*, 30:7.

Brecht, Bertolt. 1964. *Brecht on Theatre: The Development of an Aesthetic*, trans. John Willett. New York: Hill and Wang.

Brook, Peter. 1968. *The Empty Stage*. Harmondsworth: Penguin.

Brooks, Cleanth. 1949. 'The Heresy of Paraphrase', in *The Well-Wrought Urn*. London: Dennis Dobson.

Brooks, Peter. 1984. *Reading for the Plot: Design and Intention in Narrative*. Oxford: Clarendon.

Burnside, John. 2006. *A Lie About My Father*. London: Jonathan Cape.

Byron, George Gordon. 1986. *The Oxford Authors Byron*, ed. Jerome J. McGann. Oxford: Oxford University Press.

Cameron, Sharon. 2009. *Thinking in Henry James*. Chicago: University of Chicago Press.

Carroll, Lewis. 1992. *Alice in Wonderland*, ed. Donald J. Gray, 2nd edn. New York: Norton.

Carver, Raymond. 1986. 'On Writing', in *Fires: Essays, Poems, Stories*. London: Picador.

Caserio, Robert L. and Clement Hawes, eds. 2012. *The Cambridge History of the English Novel*. Cambridge: Cambridge University Press.

Cavarero, Adriana. 2000. *Relating Narratives: Storytelling and Selfhood*, trans. Paul A. Kottman. London: Routledge.

Cheeke, Stephen. 2008. *Writing for Art: The Aesthetics of Ekphrasis*. Manchester: Manchester University Press.

Chude-Sokei, Louis. 2022. *Floating in a Most Peculiar Way*. Boston: Mariner Books.

Cixous, Hélène. 1998. 'Writing Blind: Conversation with the Donkey', in *Stigmata: Escaping Texts*, trans. Eric Prenowitz. London: Routledge.

Clark, Timothy. 1997. *Theory of Inspiration: Composition as a Crisis of Subjectivity in Romantic and Post-Romantic Writing*. Manchester: Manchester University Press.

Clark, Timothy. 2011. *The Cambridge Introduction to Literature and the Environment*. Cambridge: Cambridge University Press.

Cohn, Dorrit. 1978. *Transparent Minds: Narrative Modes for Presenting Consciousness in Fiction*. Princeton: Princeton University Press.

Constantine, David. 2013. *Poetry*. Oxford: Oxford University Press.

Culler, Jonathan. 2007. *The Literary in Theory*. Stanford: Stanford University Press.

Davis, Lennard J. 1983. *Factual Fictions: The Origins of the English Novel*. New York: Columbia University Press.

de Man, Paul. 1979. *Allegories of Reading: Figural Language in Rousseau, Nietzsche, Rilke, and Proust*. New Haven: Yale University Press.

de Man, Paul. 1984. 'Autobiography as De-Facement', in *The Rhetoric of Romanticism*. New York: Columbia University Press.

Defoe, Daniel. 1719. *Robinson Crusoe*. London.

Defoe, Daniel. 1722. *Moll Flanders*. London.

Deleuze, Gilles and Félix Guattari. 2013. *A Thousand Plateaus*, trans. Brian Massumi. London: Bloomsbury.

DeLillo, Don. 2010. *Point Omega*. London: Picador.

Derrida, Jacques. 1992a. *Acts of Literature*, ed. Derek Attridge. London: Routledge.

Derrida, Jacques. 1992b. 'Afterw.rds: or, at Least, Less Than a Letter about a Letter Less', trans. Geoffrey Bennington, in *Afterwords*, ed. Nicholas Royle. Tampere, Finland: Outside Books.

Derrida, Jacques. 1995a. *On the Name*, ed. Thomas Dutoit. Stanford: Stanford University Press.

Derrida, Jacques. 1995b. ' "There is No *One* Narcissism"(Autobiophotographies)', trans. Peggy Kamuf, in *Points . . . Interviews, 1974–1994*, ed. Elisabeth Weber. London: Routledge.

Desmond, John. 2004. 'Flannery O'Connor's Misfit and the Mystery of Evil', *Renascence: Essays on Values in Literature*, 56:2, 129–137.

Dickens, Charles. 2003. *Oliver Twist, or, The Parish Boy's Progress*, ed. Philip Horner. London: Penguin.

Dickinson, Emily. 1975. *The Complete Poems of Emily Dickinson*, ed. Thomas H. Johnson. London: Faber and Faber.

Edmundson, Mark. 1990. *Towards Reading Freud: Self-Creation in Milton, Wordsworth, Emerson and Sigmund Freud*. Princeton: Princeton University Press.

Einhaus, Anne-Marie, ed. 2016. *The Cambridge Companion to the English Short Story*. Cambridge: Cambridge University Press.

Eliot, T.S. 1963. *Collected Poems 1909–1962*. New York: Harcourt Brace and Company.

Eliot, T.S. 1975. *Selected Prose of T.S. Eliot*, ed. Frank Kermode. London: Faber and Faber.

Ellis, Havelock. 1911. *The World of Dreams*. London: Constable.

Ellmann, Maud. 2010. *The Nets of Modernism: Henry James, Virginia Woolf, James Joyce, and Sigmund Freud*. Cambridge: Cambridge University Press.

Emerson, Ralph Waldo. 1996. 'The American Scholar (An Oration delivered before the Phi Beta Kappa Society, at Cambridge, Massachusetts,

August 31, 1837)', in *Essays and Poems*. New York: Library of America College Editions.

Empson, William. 2004. *Seven Types of Ambiguity*, 2nd edn. London: Pimlico.

Fabb, Nigel and Alan Durant. 2005. *How to Write Essays and Dissertations: A Guide for English Literature Students*, 2nd edn. Harlow: Pearson Longman.

Fenton, James. 2003. *An Introduction to English Poetry*. London: Penguin.

Ferrante, Elena. 2022. *In the Margins: On the Pleasures of Reading and Writing*, trans. Ann Goldstein. London: Europa Editions.

Fischer, Gerhard and Greiner Bernhard, eds. 2007. *The Play within the Play: The Performance of Meta-Theatre and Self-Reflection*. Amsterdam: Rodopi.

Fitzgerald, Edward. 2009. *Rubáiyát of Omar Khayyám*, ed. Daniel Karlin. Oxford: Oxford University Press.

Fletcher, Angus. 2023. *Storythinking: The New Science of Narrative Intelligence*. New York: Columbia University Press.

Forbes, Peter. 2009. *Dazzled and Deceived: Mimicry and Camouflage*. New Haven: Yale University Press.

Forster, E.M. 1976. *Aspects of the Novel* (1927), ed. Oliver Stallybrass. Harmondsworth: Penguin.

Freud, Sigmund. 1985. 'Creative Writers and Day-Dreaming' (1908), trans. James Strachey et al., in *The Pelican Freud Library*, ed. Albert Dickson, vol. 14. Harmondsworth: Penguin.

Freud, Sigmund. 1997. *Writings on Art and Literature*. With a Foreword by Neil Hertz. Stanford: Stanford University Press.

Freud, Sigmund. 2002. 'Analysis Terminable and Interminable' (1937), trans. Alan Bance, in *Wild Analysis*. London: Penguin.

Freud, Sigmund. 2003. 'The Uncanny' (1919), trans. David McLintock, in *The Uncanny*, ed. Adam Phillips. London: Penguin.

Fuchs, Elinor. 2004. 'EF's Visit to a Small Planet: Some Questions to Ask a Play', *Theatre*, 34:2, 4–9.

Furniss, Tom and Michael Bath. 2022. *Reading Poetry: An Introduction*, 3rd edn. London: Longman.

Garber, Marjorie. 2003. *A Manifesto for Literary Studies*. Seattle: University of Washington Press.

Ghosh, Amitav. 2016. *The Great Derangement: Climate Change and the Unthinkable*. Chicago: University of Chicago Press.

Giggs, Rebecca. 2020. *Fathoms: The World in the Whale*. London: Scribe.

Gourgouris, Stathis. 2003. *Does Literature Think? Literature as Theory for an Antimythical Era*. Stanford: Stanford University Press.

Grant, Ben. 2016. *The Aphorism and Other Short Forms*. London: Routledge.

Greenblatt, Stephen. 1988. *Shakespearean Negotiations*. Berkeley: University of California Press.

Groden, Michael and Martin Kreiswirth, eds. 2005. *The Johns Hopkins Guide to Literary Theory and Criticism*. Baltimore: Johns Hopkins University Press.

Guillory, John. 2022. *Professing Criticism: Essays on the Organization of Literary Study*. Chicago: University of Chicago Press.

Hawthorn, Jeremy. 2022. *Studying the Novel*, 8th edn. London: Bloomsbury.

Heffernan, James W. 2004. *The Poetics of Ekphrasis from Homer to Ashbery*. Chicago: University of Chicago Press.

Heidegger, Martin. 1968. *What Is Called Thinking?* trans. J. Glenn Gray. New York: Harper and Row.

Heidegger, Martin. 1975. 'The Thinker as Poet', in *Poetry, Language, Thought*, trans. Albert Hofstadter. New York: Harper Colophon Books.

Heidegger, Martin. 1976. *Early Greek Thinking: The Dawn of Western Philosophy*, trans. David Farrell Krell and Frank A. Capuzzi. New York: Harper Collins.

Hemingway, Ernest. 2003. *A Farewell to Arms*. New York: Scribner.

Hemingway, Ernest. 2011. *A Moveable Feast: The Restored Edition*. London: Random House.

Herbert, George. 2007. *The English Poems of George Herbert*, ed. Helen Wilcox. Cambridge: Cambridge University Press.

Hill, Geoffrey. 2002. *The Orchards of Syon*. London: Penguin.

Hoare, Philip. 2017. *Risingtidefallingstar*. London: 4th Estate.

Høeg, Mette Leonard, ed. 2021. *Literary Theories of Uncertainty*. London: Bloomsbury.

Hughes, Ted. 2003. *Collected Poems*, ed. Paul Keegan. New York: Farrar, Straus and Giroux.

Hunter, Adrian. 2007. *The Cambridge Introduction to the Short Story in English*. Cambridge: Cambridge University Press.

Hurley, Michael D. and Michael O'Neill. 2012. *Poetic Form: An Introduction*. Cambridge: Cambridge University Press.

Ingman, Heather. 2009. *A History of the Irish Short Story*. Cambridge: Cambridge University Press.

Ishiguro, Kazuo. 2005. *Never Let Me Go*. London: Faber and Faber.

Jordan, Julia. 2010. *Chance and the Modern British Novel: From Henry Green to Iris Murdoch*. London: Continuum.

Joyce, James. 1963. *Stephen Hero*. New York: New Directions.

Kafka, Franz. 1992. 'The Metamorphosis and A Hunger Artist', trans. Muir Willa and Edwin Muir, in *The Complete Short Stories*, ed. Nabu N. Glatzer. London: Minerva.

Kafka, Franz. 1994. *The Collected Aphorisms*, trans. Malcolm Pasley. London: Penguin.

Kahn, Andrew. 2021. *The Short Story: A Very Short Introduction*. Oxford: Oxford University Press.

Kalof, Linda and Amy J. Fitzgerald. 2007. *The Animals Reader: The Essential Classic and Contemporary Writings*. Oxford: Berg.

Kastan, Leonard. 2001. 'What Did Shakespeare Read?' in *The Cambridge Companion to Shakespeare*, eds. Margreta de Grazia and Stanley Wells. Cambridge: Cambridge University Press.

Kearney, Richard. 2002. *On Stories*. London: Routledge.

Keats, John. 1988. *The Complete Poems*, ed. John Barnard, 3rd edn. London: Penguin.

Keats, John. 2005. *Selected Letters of John Keats*, ed. Hyder Edward Rollins and Grant F. Scott. Harvard: University of Harvard Press.

Kennedy, David. n.d. 'Essay Guide', www.rlf.org.uk/fellowshipscheme/writing/essayguide.cfm.

Kermode, Frank. 1966. *The Sense of an Ending: Studies in the Theory of Fiction*. New York: Oxford University Press.

Kermode, Frank. 1985. *Forms of Attention*. Chicago: University of Chicago Press.

Knabb, Ken, ed. 2006. *Situationist International Anthology*, Revised and expanded edn, trans. Ken Knabb. Berkeley: Bureau of Public Secrets.

Larkin, Philip. 2012. *The Complete Poems*, ed. Archie Burnett. New York: Farrar, Straus and Giroux.

Lawrence, D.H. 1972. 'Why the Novel Matters', in *Phoenix: The Posthumous Papers of D. H. Lawrence*, ed. Edward D. McDonald. New York: Viking Press.

Lennard, John. 2005. *The Poetry Handbook: A Guide to Reading Poetry for Pleasure and Practical Criticism*, 2nd edn. Oxford: Oxford University Press.

Lodge, David. 2002. *Consciousness and the Novel*. Cambridge, MA: Harvard University Press.

Mabey, Richard. 1995. *The Oxford Book of Nature Writing*. Oxford: Oxford University Press.

Macdonald, Helen. 2014. *H is for Hawk*. London: Jonathan Cape.

Macdonald, Helen. 2020. *Vesper Flights: New and Collected Essays*. London: Jonathan Cape.

Macfarlane, Robert. 2012. *The Old Ways: A Journey on Foot*. London: Penguin.

Macfarlane, Robert. 2014. 'Introduction to Nan Shepherd', in *The Living Mountain*. Edinburgh: Canongate.

Macherey, Pierre. 2006. *A Theory of Literary Production*, trans. Geoffrey Wall. Abingdon: Routledge.

MacLeish, Archibald. 1963. *The Collected Poems*. Boston: Houghton Mifflin.

Mahony, Patrick J. 1987. *Freud as a Writer*, Expanded edn. New Haven: Yale University Press.

Malcolm, Cheryl Alexander and David Malcolm, eds. 2008. *A Companion to the British and Irish Short Story*. Chichester: Wiley-Blackwell.

Mallarmé, Stephane. 1994. *Collected Poems*, trans. Henry Weinfield. Berkeley: University of California Press.

Mantel, Hilary. 2003. *Giving Up the Ghost: A Memoir*. London: Fourth Estate.

March-Russell. Paul. 2012. *The Short Story: An Introduction*. Edinburgh: Edinburgh University Press.

Marcus, Laura. 2018. *Autobiography: A Very Short Introduction*. Oxford: Oxford University Press.

Maunder, Andrew, et al. 2011. *The British Short Story*. Basingstoke: Palgrave Macmillan.

Maxwell, Glyn. 2012. *On Poetry*. London: Oberon Books.

May, Charles E. 1994. *The New Short Story Theories*. Athens, OH: Ohio University Press.

McGurl, Mark. 2009. *The Program Era: Postwar Fiction and the Rise of Creative Writing*. Cambridge, MA: Harvard University Press.

McGurl, Mark. 2021. *Everything and Less: The Novel in the Age of Amazon*. London: Verso.

McKeon, Michael. 1987. *The Origins of the English Novel*, 1600–1740. Baltimore: Johns Hopkins University Press.

Meisel, Perry. 2007. *The Literary Freud*. London: Routledge.

Merleau-Ponty, Maurice. 1964. *Signs*, trans. Richard McCleary. Evanston, IL: Northwestern University Press.

Merleau-Ponty, Maurice. 2012. *Phenomenology of Perception*, trans. Donald A. Landes. London: Routledge.

Miller, J. Hillis. 2002. *On Literature*. London and New York: Routledge.

Milton, John. 2003. *The Major Works*, eds. Stephen Orgel and Jonathan Goldberg. Oxford: Oxford University Press.

Mitchell, W.J.T. 1986. *Iconology: Image, Text, Ideology*. Chicago: University of Chicago Press.

Mitchell, W.J.T. 1994. *Picture Theory: Essays on Verbal and Visual Representation*. Chicago: University of Chicago Press.

Mitchell, W.J.T. 2005. *What Do Pictures Want? The Lives and Loves of Images*. Chicago: University of Chicago Press.

Montaigne, Michel de. 2003. *The Complete Essays*, trans. M.A. Screech. London: Penguin.

Morris, Pam. 2003. *Realism*. London: Routledge.

Morton, Timothy. 2007. *Ecology without Nature: Rethinking Environmental Aesthetics*. Cambridge, MA: Harvard University Press.

Morton, Timothy. 2010. *The Ecological Thought*. Cambridge, MA: Harvard University Press.

Newlyn, Lucy. 2021. *The Craft of Poetry: A Primer in Verse*. New Haven, CT: Yale University Press.

Nietzsche, Friedrich. 1997. *Daybreak: Thoughts on the Prejudices of Morality*, eds. Maudemarie Clark and Brian Leiter. Cambridge: Cambridge University Press.

Noreen Masud. 2023. *Stevie Smith and the Aphorism: Hard Language*. Oxford: Oxford University Press.

North, Michael. 2013. *Novelty: A History of the New*. Chicago: Chicago University Press.

O'Connor, Flannery. 2009. *Complete Stories*. London: Faber and Faber.

O'Connor, Frank. 1963. *The Lonely Voice: A Study of the Short Story*. Cleveland: World Publishing.

Orwell, George. 1968. 'The Frontiers of Art and Propaganda', in *The Collected Essays, Journalism, and Letters of George Orwell*, vol. 2. London: Secker and Warburg.

Orwell, George. 2009. *Nineteen Eighty-Four*. London: Penguin.

Pascal, Blaise. 1995. *Pensées and Other Writings*, trans. Honor Levi. Oxford: Oxford University Press.

Peck, John and Martin Coyle. 2012. *The Student's Guide to Writing: Spelling, Punctuation and Grammar*, 3rd edn. Basingstoke: Palgrave Macmillan.

Phillips, Adam. 2006. 'Introduction', in *The Penguin Freud Reader*, ed. Adam Phillips. London: Penguin.

Pirandello, Luigi. 1985. 'Six Characters in Search of an Author', in *Three Plays: The Rules of the Game, Six Characters in Search of an Author, Henry IV*, trans. Robert Rietty, Noel Cregeen, John Linstrum and Julian Mitchell. London: Methuen.

Poe, Edgar Allan. 1965. 'Twice-Told Tales. By Nathaniel Hawthorne', in *The Complete Works of Edgar Allan Poe*, ed. James A. Harrison, vol. XI. New York: AMS Press.

Poole, Adrian. 2005. *Tragedy: A Very Short Introduction*. Oxford: Oxford University Press.

Pope, Alexander. 2006. *The Major Works*, ed. Pat Rogers. Oxford: Oxford University Press.

Pritchett, V.S. 1982. *Collected Stories*. London: Chatto and Windus.

Prynne, J.H. 2010. 'Poetic Thought', *Textual Practice*, 24:4, 595–606.

Quinn, Arthur. 2010. *Figures of Speech: 60 Ways to Turn a Phrase*. London: Routledge.

Rapaport, Herman. 2011. *The Literary Theory Toolkit: A Compendium of Concepts and Methods*. Oxford: Wiley-Blackwell.

Readings, Bill. 1991. *Introducing Lyotard: Arts and Politics*. London: Routledge.

Readings, Bill. 1996. *The University in Ruins*. Cambridge, MA: Harvard University Press.

Richardson, Brian. 2006. *Unnatural Voices: Extreme Narration in Modern and Contemporary Fiction*. Columbus: Ohio State University Press.

Rimbaud, Jean Nicolas Arthur. 1966. *Complete Works, Selected Letters*, trans. Wallace Fowlie. Chicago: Chicago University Press.

Ronell, Avital. 2002. *Stupidity*. Champaign: University of Illinois Press.

Royle, Nicholas. 2014. *How to Read Shakespeare*, New edn. London: Granta.

Royle, Nicholas. 2020. *Hélène Cixous: Dreamer, Realist, Analyst, Writing*. Manchester: Manchester University Press.

Ryan, Vanessa Lyndal. 2012. *Thinking Without Thinking in the Victorian Novel*. Baltimore: Johns Hopkins University Press.

Sage, Lorna. 2000. *Bad Blood*. London: Fourth Estate.

Scofield, Martin. 2006. *The Cambridge Introduction to the American Short Story*. Cambridge: Cambridge University Press.

Shakespeare, William. 2000. *Romeo and Juliet*, ed. Jill L. Levenson. Oxford: Oxford University Press.

Shelley, Percy Bysshe. 1977. *Shelley's Poetry and Prose*, ed. Donald H. Reiman and Sharon B. Powers. New York: Norton.

Shepherd, Nan. 2014. *The Living Mountain*. Edinburgh: Canongate.

Singer, Margot and Nicole Walker, eds. 2023. *Bending Genre: Essays on Creative Nonfiction*, 2nd edn. London: Bloomsbury.

Sterne, Laurence. 2003. *The Life and Opinions of Tristram Shandy, Gentleman*, eds. Melvyn New and Joan New. London: Penguin.

Stevens, Wallace. 1951. *The Necessary Angel: Essays on Reality and the Imagination*. New York: Knopf.

Stevens, Wallace. 1997. *Collected Poetry and Prose*. New York: Library of America.

Storm, William. 2011. *Irony and the Modern Theatre*. Cambridge: Cambridge University Press.

Strachan, John and Richard Terry. 2011. *Poetry*, 2nd edn. Edinburgh: Edinburgh University Press.

Tambling, Jeremy. 2012. *Literature and Psychoanalysis*. Manchester: Manchester University Press.

Tate, Gregory. 2012. *The Poet's Mind: The Psychology of Victorian Poetry, 1830–1870*. Oxford: Oxford University Press.

Tennyson, Alfred. 1989. *Tennyson: A Selected Edition*, ed. Christopher Ricks. Harlow: Longman.

Uhlmann, Anthony. 2011. *Thinking in Literature: Joyce, Woolf, Nabokov*. New York: Continuum.

Walcott, Derek. 1997. *The Bounty*. London: Faber and Faber.

Wallace, David Foster. 1998. 'E Unibus Pluram: Television and US Fiction', in *A Supposedly Fun Thing I'll Never Do Again: Essays and Arguments*. London: Abacus.

Wallace, David Foster. 2000. *Brief Interviews with Hideous Men*. London: Abacus.

Wallace, David Foster. 2005. *Everything and More: A Compact History of Infinity*. London: Orion Books.

Wallace, David Foster. 2011. *The Pale King*. London: Hamish Hamilton.

Wallace, David Foster. 2012. *Conversations with David Foster Wallace*, ed. Stephen J. Burn. Jackson: University Press of Mississippi.

Wallace, Jennifer. 2007. *The Cambridge Introduction to Tragedy*. Cambridge: Cambridge University Press.

Watt, Ian. 1957. *The Rise of the Novel: Studies in Defoe, Richardson, and Fielding*. London: Chatto & Windus.

Wilde, Oscar. 2013. *De Profundis and Other Prison Writings*, ed. Colm Tóibín. London: Penguin.

Williams, Raymond. 1983. *Keywords: A Vocabulary of Culture and Society*, Revised edn. London: Fontana.

Wimsatt, W.K. 1954. *The Verbal Icon: Studies in the Meaning of Poetry*. Lexington: University of Kentucky Press.

Wittgenstein, Ludwig. 1961. *Tractatus Logico-Philosophicus*, trans. D.F. Pears and B.F. McGuinness. London: Routledge and Kegan Paul.

Wittgenstein, Ludwig. 1997. *Philosophical Investigations*, trans. G.E.M. Anscombe, 2nd edn. Oxford: Blackwell.

Woolf, Virginia. 2002. 'A Sketch of the Past', in *Moments of Being: Autobiographical Writings*, ed. Jeanne Schulkind, introduced and revised by Hermione Lee. London: Pimlico.

Wordsworth, William. 2010. *William Wordsworth*, ed. Stephen Gill. Oxford: Oxford University Press.

Yeats, W.B. 1940. *Letters on Poetry from W.B. Yeats to Dorothy Wellesley*. London: Oxford University Press.

Zunshine, Lisa. 2010. *Introduction to Cognitive Cultural Studies*. Baltimore: Johns Hopkins University Press.

Index

adaptation (TV and film) 47, 61
alienation effect 47, 148
anaphora 31, 148
animals 82–83, 130–131, 143
anthropocentrism 81
aphorism 103–105, 148
aposiopesis 69, 149
Aristotle: *Poetics* 31, 41, 140
Atwood, Margaret 12
Auden, W.H.: '1 September 1939'
    28; 'Funeral Blues' 26–27, 32;
    'In Memory of W.B. Yeats' 10;
    'Musée des Beaux Arts' 22–32
Augustine, St: *Confessions* 73
Austen, Jane 43–45; *Persuasion*
    44–45, 47; *Pride and Prejudice*
    29–30
Austin, J.L. 74, 110
authorship 30, 130–131
autobiography 73, 77; *see also* memoir

Baker, J.A. 84–85; *The Peregrine*
    80–84
Barthes, Roland 13, 152; *Camera*
    Lucida 137
Bateson, Gregory 99
Beckett, Samuel 80; *Company*
    7; *Endgame* 68, 69, 70,

72–73; 'Stirrings Still' 7; *The*
    Unnamable 7; *Waiting for Godot*
    98; *Watt* 125
Benjamin, Walter: 'The
    Storyteller' 138
Bible 54, 56, 73, 105
Bishop, Elizabeth: 'The Moose'
    143
Blanchot, Maurice: *The Space of*
    Literature 7
Bloom, Harold 66
Bolaño, Robert: *2666* 11
Bowen, Elizabeth 50–51, 57, 105,
    139, 140; *The Hotel* 102; *The*
    Little Girls 35–36
Bowie, David 74
Boxall, Peter 84
Brecht, Bertolt 47
Brooks, Cleanth 28
Brooks, Peter 142
Brown, Natasha: *Assembly* 50
Brueghel, Pieter: *Landscape with the*
    Fall of Icarus 25–26, 31
Buckeridge, Anthony 41
Burnside, John: *A Lie About My*
    Father 77
Byron, George Gordon: *Don*
    Juan 67

Carroll, Lewis: *Alice in Wonderland* 6
Carver, Raymond 141; 'On
    Writing' 142
chance 5, 24, 65, 67–68, 70, 71
character 66–67
Chekhov, Anton 138
Chude-Sokei, Louis: *Floating in a
    Most Peculiar Way* 74
Cixous, Hélène: 'Writing
    Blind' 125
Clark, Timothy 9, 81, 83, 84, 133
close reading 22, 32, 69, 109, 119
Cohn, Dorrit 42, 102
coincidence 4–5, 67, 70
conclusions 119–120
confession 73–74
Connell, Evan 142
Conrad, Joseph: *Heart of
    Darkness* 50
Coover, Robert: 'The
    BabySitter' 142
creative reading 15–18, 28, 134, 149

death 11–12, 96–98, 138
deconstruction 138, 150; *see also*
    Jacques Derrida
Defoe, Daniel: *Moll Flanders* 38,
    40–41, 47; *Robinson Crusoe*
    38–39, 41, 47
DeLillo, Don: *Point Omega* 4–5
de Man, Paul 77
Derrida, Jacques 11, 31, 77, 138,
    149, 152
desire 70
Dickens, Charles 17; *Oliver Twist*
    2, 3–4
Dickinson, Emily: 'I'm Nobody!
    Who are you?' 2–3, 4
dictionaries 145–147
Dostoevsky, Fyodor 134
double bind 99, 150
Douglas, Frederick: *Narrative of the
    Life of Frederick Douglas* 41

dreams 8–9, 133–134
Dury, Ian 115

ecology *see* environment
ekphrasis 24, 28, 32, 150–151
elegy 27, 151
Eliot, T.S.: 'Philip Massinger' 116;
    The Waste Land 17, 101–102
Ellis, Bret Easton: *American
    Psycho* 11
Ellis, Havelock 133
Ellmann, Maud: *The Nets of
    Modernism* 106–110
Emerson, Ralph Waldo: 'The
    American Scholar' 17, 18
endings 142
environment 9, 72–73, 78–79,
    84, 109
epiphany 51, 53, 140, 151
epistolary 36, 117, 151
essay questions 117–118, 120–121
exemplarity 28, 31, 33

Faulkner, William: *Absolom,
    Absolom!* 11
fiction 5–6, 37–42
Fitzgerald, Edward: *Rubáiyát of
    Omar Khayyám* 11–12
focalization 48, 151
Forbes, Peter 14
formalism 9
Forster, E.M.: *Aspects of the Novel*
    76, 117
Four Weddings and a Funeral 26
free indirect discourse 45, 151
Freud, Sigmund 108, 130, 132,
    135; *Beyond the Pleasure
    Principle* 3, 150; 'Creative
    Writing and Day Dreaming'
    133–134; 'Humour' 137–138

Ghosh, Amitav 9
Gordimer, Nadine 53

Goya, Francisco: 'Disasters of War' 26
Green, Eddie 54
Greenblatt, Stephen 12

Hazanavicius, Michael: *The Artist* 94–95
Hazlitt, William: 'Characters of Shakespeare's Plays' 63, 65
Heidegger, Martin 105
Hemingway, Ernest: *A Farewell to Arms* 14–15; *A Movable Feast* 138, 139; 'Out of Season' 141
Herbert, George: 'Affliction (I)' 130; 'Easter Wings' 93–94
Hill, Geoffrey 122
Hoare, Philip 83
Hughes, Ted 80–81; *Birthday Letters* 117; 'Hawk Roosting' 130–131
Hughes, Thomas: *Tom Brown's School Days* 41
humour 137–138
Hunter, Adrian 50
Huxley, Aldous: *Brave New World* 37
Hval, Jenny: *Girls Against God* 11

Ibsen, Henrik: *Hedda Gabler* 69
imagination 8
intentionality 30, 32
interiority 42–45, 66, 75, 102
interpretation 30
intertextuality 32, 54, 58, 152
irony 30, 44, 63–64, 69, 152
Ishiguro, Kazuo: *Never Let Me Go* 41–42, 46–47

Jackson, Dennis: *The Exam Secret* 123–124
James, Henry 109, 138
Jordan, Julia 5

Josipovici, Gabriel 103
Joyce, James 51, 53; *Stephen Hero* 51

Kafka, Franz 103, 130, 139; 'The Hunger Artist' 142–143; 'The Metamorphosis' 130
Kane, Sarah: *4.48* 70
Keats, John: *Letters* 4, 62, 139; 'Ode on a Grecian Urn' 90–91, 139; 'When I have fears that I may cease to be' 91–92
Keegan, Claire: *Foster* 50
Kermode, Frank 33, 142
King, Martin Luther 10

Langland, William: *Piers Plowman* 8
Larkin, Philip: 'Aubade' 97–98
Lawrence, D.H. 17, 138; 'Why the Novel Matters' 11–12
life 11–12
literary criticism 101, 106
literary studies 6–7, 129, 136
literary theory 32, 104, 152
literature: definition of 1–2
love 67, 143
lyric poetry 42

Macdonald, Helen 82–83, 84; *H is for Hawk* 82
Macfarlane, Robert 79, 80, 85
Macherey, Pierre 37
MacLeish, Archibald: 'Ars Poetica' 28
magical thinking 12–13, 152
Mansfield, Katherine 138
Mantel, Hilary: *Giving Up the Ghost* 75–76
Marcus, Laura 75
Marx, Karl and Friedrich Engels: *Communist Manifesto* 10
McDonald's 10
Melville, Herman: *Billy Bud* 50
memoir 72–78

Merleau Ponty, Maurice 79, 135
Milton, John: 'Lycidas' 27
mimesis 14, 153
mind reading 42–45, 47, 102, 130
modernism 8, 23, 108–109
Montaigne, Michel de 115–116;
    'On Educating Children' 116,
    117, 122, 124
Morgan, Edwin 93
Morris, Pam 37
Morton, Timothy 109

Nabokov, Vladimir: *Speak,
    Memory* 14
narcissism 27, 77
narrators 44–47, 48, 58, 153
nature writing 72–73, 78–85
New Criticism 9
Newell, Mike *see Four Weddings and
    a Funeral*
Nietzsche, Friedrich: *Daybreak* 22
note taking 16, 116–117

Obama, Barack 10
O'Connor, Flannery: 'A Good
    Man is Hard to Find'
    54–57, 58
omniscient narrator 45, 153
oppositions 108–109
ordinary 13–15, 23, 32, 115
originality 115
Orwell, George 75; *Animal Farm*
    50; 'The Frontiers of Art
    and Propaganda' 99; *Nineteen
    Eighty Four* 98–99
Ovid: *Metamorphoses* 26, 130
Oxford English Dictionary 145,
    146–147

Paley, Grace 141
paradox 79–80, 99
paraphrase 28–29, 32, 153
paratexts 47, 153

Pascal, Blaise: *Pensées* 22
performativity 10, 30, 73–74, 76,
    77, 139, 154
peripeteia 140
Phillips, Adam 134
philosophy 105–106
Piers Plowman see Langland, William
Pirandello, Luigi: *Six Characters in
    Search of an Author* 131
plagiarism 116
Plath, Sylvia: 'Daddy' 117
pleasure 13, 42, 66, 95, 127, 150
Poe, Edgar Allan 50, 51, 58,
    140–141; 'The Sphinx' 141
politics 9–11, 99
Pope, Alexander: 'An Essay on
    Criticism' 103, 105
Pound, Ezra 8
Pritchett, V.S. 50, 53, 141
probability 42
prolepsis 16, 109, 154
psychoanalysis 108, 133–134;
    see also Sigmund Freud

quotations in essays 119,
    120–121, 126

Readings, Bill 28–29
realism 8, 13–15, 37–38, 41, 42
reality effect 13–15
religion, religious belief 11, 17, 51,
    54, 55, 57, 73, 97
revising essays 123, 127
rhyme 23–24, 29
Rimbaud, Arthur 105
Rowling, J. K. 41

Sartre, Jean-Paul 79
self, the 76–78
semi-colons 125
Shakespeare, William: *Hamlet* 2, 3,
    5, 42, 68, 69, 97, 146–147;
    Julius Caesar 9; *King Lear* 132;

Macbeth 42; *A Midsummer Night's Dream* 69, 134; Othello 42; *Romeo and Juliet* 60–69; *As You Like It* 8, 10, 69
Shelley, Percy Bysshe 8; 'Adonais' 27; 'To a Skylark' 84
Shepherd, Nan: *The Living Mountain* 79, 80
simulacrum 14, 155
singularity 18, 31, 33, 155
Situationists 10
soliloquy 42, 155
Sterne, Laurence: *Tristram Shandy* 18
Stevens, Wallace 143; *The Necessary Angel* 8

telepathic narrator 45, 155
Tennyson, Alfred: *In Memoriam* 27
thesis statement 123
Thoreau, Henry David 78
titles 47, 57
trauma 137, 138
TV 14, 47

university, purpose and value of 132

voice 21, 30, 47, 58, 74, 75, 85, 116, 125, 139

Walcott, Derek: *The Bounty* 27
Wallace, David Foster 47, 91; *The Pale King* 5; 'Suicide as a Sort of Present' 51–54
Waugh, Evelyn: *A Handful of Dust* 17
Welty, Eudora 141
White, Gilbert 78
Wilde, Oscar: *De Profundis* 104
Williams, Raymond 1–2
Wilson, Kabe 8
Wimsatt, W.K. 31
Wittgenstein, Ludwig: *Tractatus Logico-Philosophicus* 104–106, 109
Woolf, Virginia: *A Sketch of the Past* 73, 76
Wordsworth, William: 'The Thorn' 14–15
writer's block 131–132

Yeats, W.B. 53